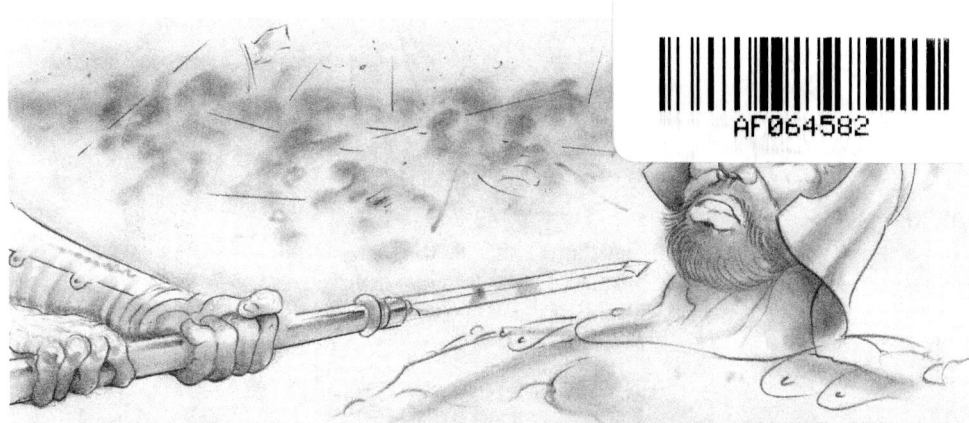

Dohrenwend's Masterwork
On the Spear, Sling, Sai, and Walking Stick

An Anthology of Articles from the *Journal of Asian Martial Arts*

Edited by Michael A. DeMarco, M.A.

Writings by Robert E. Dohrenwend, Ph.D.

Disclaimer

Please note that the authors and publisher of this book are not responsible in any manner whatsoever for any injury that may result from practicing the techniques and/or following the instructions given within. Since the physical activities described herein may be too strenuous in nature for some readers to engage in safely, it is essential that a physician be consulted prior to training.

All Rights Reserved

No part of this publication, including illustrations, may be reproduced or utilized in any form or by any means, electronic or mechanical, including photocopying, recording, or by any information storage and retrieval system (beyond that copying permitted by sections 107 and 108 of the US Copyright Law and except by reviewers for the public press), without written permission from Via Media Publishing Company.

Warning: Any unauthorized act in relation to a copyright work may result in both a civil claim for damages and criminal prosecution.

Copyright © 2015 by
Via Media Publishing Company
941 Calle Mejia #822
Santa Fe, NM 87501 USA
E-mail: md@goviamedia.com

All articles in this anthology were originally published in the *Journal of Asian Martial Arts*.
Listed according to the table of contents for this anthology:

Dohrenwend, R. (2002)   Volume 11, Number 2   pages 28–49
Dohrenwend, R. (2002)   Volume 11, Number 3   pages 8–29
Dohrenwend, R. (2005)   Volume 14, Number 4   pages 8–31
Dohrenwend, R. (2007)   Volume 16, Number 1   pages 8–35

Book and cover design by Via Media Publishing Company

Edited by Michael A. DeMarco, M.A.

Cover illustrations
by Oscar Ratti from the graphic novel series,
Tales of the Hermit, Vol. I, II, & III
published by Via Media Publishing.
Copyright by Future Designs & Publications.

ISBN: 978-1-893765-20-7

w w w . v i a m e d i a p u b l i s h i n g . c o m

contents

Preface
Michael DeMarco, M.A.

Author Bio Note

CHAPTERS

1   The Sling: Forgotten Firepower of Antiquity

24   The Odd East Asian Sai

52   The Walking Stick: The Gentlemans Weapon

86   The Spear: An Effective Weapon Since Antiquity

125   **Index**

Author's Bio Note
Robert E. Dohrenwend, Ph.D., received his Ph.D. in micrometeorology from Syracuse University and has studied various languages at the Sorbonne and other schools, both abroad and within the United States. He has been an enthusiastic hunter with the traditional longbow for over a quarter of a century, and his martial arts experience ranges from the Hungarian saber to Okinawan and Japanese karate and Korean taekwondo. He retired to write and translate in the fields of military history, weapons history, and the martial arts.

preface

When it comes to martial traditions, Dr. Robert Dohrenwend exemplifies a rare breed of scholar-warrior I have fortunately come to know over the past few decades. He is a former associate editor for the *Journal of Asian Martial Arts*, and it has been a very welcomed pleasure to work with a man who possesses both an encyclopedic depth of military traditions and a great disposition. But he is not solely a bookworm. He balances mental work with a wide variety of sweaty combatives from the four cardinal directions. For Via Media Publishing, this is a special book representing some of the best work we published in our periodical.

You will find four chapters in this book devoted to weapons that have had enormous impact on world civilization: the sling, sai, walking stick, and spear. As Dr. Dohrenwend writes, "The spear may be man's oldest purpose-made weapon." With the spear and sling, we traverse millennia of human involvement with weapon innovation for hunting and warfare. These represent our primal roots. They are still with us today.

The walking stick is normally seen as a practical device made to assist in walking and hiking. As a weapon, there's much more to a cane than meets the eye. It can help portray a gentlemanly air when "worn" with dapper clothing, as popular in the late nineteenth and early twentieth centuries. For civilian self-defense, it is convenient and effective.

Many are familiar with the Okinawan sai, but may be unaware that the weapon exists in other geographic areas as well. Did these evolve from some farming tool? Dohrenwend thinks not. We have some solid references for the sai, including written and oral records, plus material artifacts. Much more needs to be done to fill in the overall picture of the weapon's place in history.

In each chapter Dr. Dohrenwend utilizes his academic research and practical experience to give the most complete overview of the weapons. This includes not only their history, but other aspects such as their purpose, design, effectiveness, cost of production, and uses in military and civilian settings. There is much to absorb: scientific data and analyses, fighting techniques, stories, and some humor. Dohrenwend's efforts produce quality reading, now conveniently assembled here. There's no doubt this book will be a standard reference for these formidable weapons.

Michael A. DeMarco, Publisher
Santa Fe, New Mexico
November 2015

The Sling:
Forgotten Firepower of Antiquity

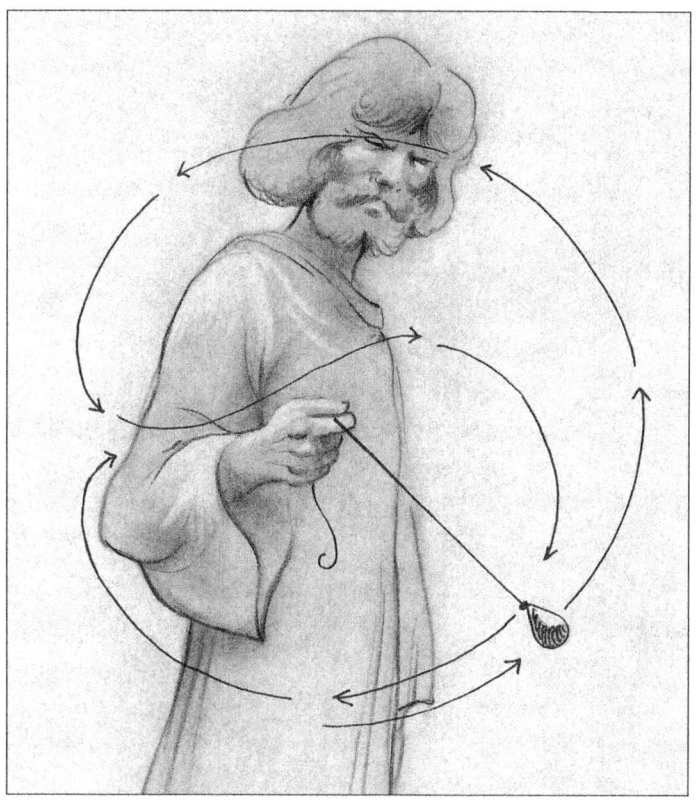

Illustration courtesy of Oscar Ratti. © 2001 Futuro Designs & Publications.

Introduction

The sling was an important military weapon from the beginnings of organized warfare to the end of the Middle Ages. However, although it is one of the most effective missile weapons ever devised, it is generally neglected by military historians, receiving brief mention only in the most general terms when it appears at all. Detailed discussion of the sling has been relegated to a specialist literature that is both sparse and not easily available. This is all the more surprising when we consider the enormous literature dealing with the military use of archery. According to the few available studies, the sling out-ranged the bow, was more accurate, and easily as deadly. A sling can throw a lethal projectile almost a quarter of a mile, and in the hands of an expert, it is very accurate at distances up to a least 220 yards. Both the weapon and its ammunition are very inexpensive.

There are two basic types of sling: the hand sling and the staff sling. The staff sling seems to have been almost exclusively a military weapon, and was much less common than the hand sling. Although it has a very respectable antiquity, it would seem that it was less accurate and less powerful than the hand sling. We will not discuss the staff sling in the following discussion.

Historical Background

According to Ferrill (1985: 240), the sling appeared between 12,000 and 8,000 BCE. Other sources are more vague and only state sometime before 6,000 BCE. Anthropologist V. Gordon Childe demonstrated that a useful criterion for the division of Mediterranean Neolithic culture provinces is the choice of missile weapon, the exclusive use of either sling or bow (1951: 1–5). In Egypt, the sling appears only at the beginning of the XXth dynasty (1187–1069 BCE) in the new kingdom (Yadim, 1963: 83). Apparently, choice of one precluded the development of skill or even interest in the other. There appears to have been no selective advantage of one over the other.

Slings appeared in Assyrian armies only in the 8th century BCE in the reign of Tiglathpileser II (or possibly III), with the slingers operating in pairs behind the archers (Yadim, 1963: 296). The archers were the main combat arm of the Assyrian infantry, which used an advanced type of composite bow.

Sources describing the military use of the sling at later dates (i.e. Persian and Assyrian armies) often describe slingers as brigaded and deployed with archers in battle. Xenophon (1959: 78–79) is remarkable for the detail in which he discusses slingers; other ancient sources are less useful.

Assyrian Slingers and a Greek Cavalryman

Charcoal drawings by Oscar Ratti.

© Copyright 2002 by Futuro Design & Publications.

In the Roman Republic, there were regular cohorts of slingers (Ferrill, 1985: 26). In the same period, "The Visigoths are said to have been excellent slingers" (De Hoffmayer, 1982: 89). Balearic slingers were used as mercenaries until the end of the medieval period (Korfmann, 1972: 7). Although slingers had less status in ancient armies than did heavy infantry, this does not necessarily reflect on their utility.

Slings were used in European armies until the 16th century, at which time they were often used to throw glowing coals and grenades (Demmin, 1893: 875). Heinrich VII's (1308–1313) expedition to Italy was accompanied by slingers. The Castilians used slings at Nájera (1367); Froissart (1901: 108) claims that they smashed in helms and bassinets. Froissart also asserts that the Castilian king had 30,000 infantry slingers in 1386 (De Hoffmayer, 1982: 213). Many slingshots were found at the site of the Battle of   (1385) (Reid, 1976: 21). The sling was last used in Europe for military purposes at the siege of Sancerre in 1572 by the Huguenots. These Huguenot slings were nicknamed *arquebuses de Sancerre* (Reid, 1976: 21). In Peru and Mexico, the Aztecs and Incas made very effective use of slings against the Spanish conquistadores (Mahr, 1964: 123; Friedrici, 1910: 289). The people's party during the minority of Louis XIV called themselves *La Fronde* (The Sling) in their contest against Anne of Austria and Cardinal Mazarin (Demmin, 1893: 875; Korfmann, 1972: 7).

In Asia, the sling was generally used by tribal peoples outside the direct influence of civilization centers. Normally these were pastoral peoples and, in fact, the weapon is often called the "shepherd's bow." This is especially true for East and Central Asia, where the sling was in recent use in Tajikistan, Kyrgyzstan, Afghanistan, the Indian mountains, the southern half of the Malaysian Peninsula, Guangdong Province in China, and Korea. It is also known in Indonesia and the Philippines. In Tibet, it was in regular military use up to the end of the last century, and the Tibetans were reported to be able to throw a stone 300 yards with one. Sir Aurel Stein found a sling in the Tsaidam Basin area, which is said to date from the 9th century C.E., and the weapon was in recent use by the Mongols in that area (Lindblom, 1940: 33–35).

In Europe, the sling was used in more modern times as a shepherd's weapon: in Dalmatia (18th and 19th centuries), the Alps (up to the 20th), England (up to the 19th), and the Balearic Islands (to the present) (Korfmann, 1972: 7). It is still in use in Spain, Syria, Palestine, Jordan, the Hejaz, north Africa, and the Canary Islands (Korfmann, 1972: 7). During the Spanish Civil War, at the Siege of Alcázar (Toledo), Loyalists threw grenades into the fortress with slings (Korfmann, 1973: 41).

The sling has been used as a hunting weapon, but it was more commonly used for protecting crops and livestock. Although there are pictures showing the weapon used to throw stones at birds in flight, it is not certain whether the birds were being hunted or merely chased away from gardens or fields. The accuracy required is very different for the two purposes.

Most of the technical information available on slings comes from studies of the weapon as used in Europe or by primitive societies during the period of initial contact with Europeans. There are very few studies of this weapon as used in East or Central Asia, but its technical features and the analysis of its use as presented here should apply to all cultures. Like archery, the practical use of the sling was drastically curtailed by the introduction of modern firearms. Unlike archery with its enormous modern following, the use of the sling has not become a 20th century sport.

Modern sling made of leather, cord, and brass grommets.
Courtesy of R. Dohrenwend.

Description

The sling is one of the simplest of all weapons to make and its ammunition is extremely easy to make or find. Korfmann makes the point that slings were mostly found in areas where proper-sized stones and pebbles were readily available (1972: 10). The weapon consists of two strings connected to a pouch between them. The free end of one string has a loop or knot to keep it from sliding off the hand while the other end may either be left free to facilitate release or provided with a knot to increase control.

The sling may be made of a wide variety of substances. Plaited grass and a variety of woven materials have been used (Hawkins, 1847: 98; Lindblom, 1940: 7, 33–35; Mahr, 1964: 119; Korfmann, 1972: 4–5) and leather and wool were also common materials (Mahr, 1964: 119). Some slings were made of a single piece of leather for increased strength.

It is difficult to improve on the basic sling. Possibilities for doing so are limited to: (a) form of the projectile; (b) the length of the thongs, straps, or strings; or (c) superior materials and craftsmanship.

Throwing Techniques

The throwing techniques control the initial velocity at departure of the missile from the sling (departure velocity) and the angle of departure. Departure velocity is determined by the length of the path over which acceleration occurs, the uniformity of acceleration along that path, and the acceleration itself. The angle of departure is unaffected by departure velocity. We will examine three basic throwing techniques:

1) Whirling the sling in a horizontal plane around a vertical axis extending from the ground up through the top of the head (around the head). After placing the stone (or other projectile) in the sling's pouch, the sling is raised above the slinger's head with the pouch held in the left hand, and the ends of the strings in the right hand. The pouch is released with a small toss to the side, and then whirled around the head with the right hand. The initial whirl is done with the wrist; at the second (or final) whirl, the arm straightens involving the elbow and shoulder. This accelerates the rotational speed while increasing the length of the arc described by the sling's pouch. At the proper moment, the end of one string is released. The pouch opens, and the projectile flies toward its target (Yadim, 1963: 364).

   The projectile reaches its maximum velocity very quickly. Romans were trained to release projectiles at the sling's first turn (Ferrill, 1985: 36). Apparently, three revolutions to gain speed before release was considered normal elsewhere. Further revolutions add very little additional velocity at an unacceptable cost in muscular exhaustion. All other factors being equal, the velocity for a particular sling will be determined by its length, which determines the length of the path over which the projectile accelerates.

2) Whirling the sling in a vertical plane initially around a horizontal axis extending parallel to the ground through the wrist, then involving the entire arm for power in the final rotation. Once again, the projectile reaches its maximum velocity very quickly (two revolutions); and, all other factors being equal, the velocity for a particular sling will be determined by its length. Depending on the direction of rotation, the projectile may be released at either

the top or bottom of the swing. If the release is at the bottom of the swing, it is difficult to involve the entire arm for power unless the sling is relatively short. Otherwise, it will strike the ground before release. This technique does not seem as strong as the first.

3) Beginning with the sling pouch containing the projectile on the ground in front of the slinger, the sling is whipped backwards and up behind the slinger to describe a complex, curved, vertical path that arcs upwards. As it descends, the sling is given a straight, sidearm acceleration toward the target. This technique is somewhat similar to cracking a whip, and imparts a greater acceleration to the projectile than the two techniques described above, and gives the greatest height and distance. This technique may also be adapted to an overhand throw (Blaine, 1960: 31–34).

Throwing sequence as described above in number 3.
Illustrations by Oscar Ratti. © 2002 by Futuro Design & Publications.

There is no standardization of throwing techniques, so others are possible and some techniques have been described that appear to be recent developments (Savage, 1984: 39–44). These seem to be more involved or weaker than those described above and would seem to be less suitable for military applications where maximum range and impact are required. They might possibly have applications for close work, throwing from cover, rapid response, or closer accuracy. Or they might not.

SLING BALLISTICS

Projectiles

These vary widely in size, shape, and materials; and include smooth stones, egg-shaped stones, limestone, sun-dried clay ovoids and biconical projectiles, and cast lead. Missiles were originally spherical, becoming biconical, and then ovoid or egg-shaped after 4,000 BCE (Korfmann, 1973: 38). Near Eastern projectile dimensions vary from 0.5 to 6.5 ounces; 0.3 to 4 inches (diameters of 0.8 to 2 inches) (Korfmann, 1973: 38). A lead Greek sling stone had twice the range of the heavy stones used by the Persians (Warry, 1980: 62). Lindblom states that the Greeks used lead as early as the 5th century (1940: 9). Balearic slingers were known to use heavier projectiles than normal. Stones were used during the Roman Empire, while lead was used during the Republic (Watson, 1969: 61). It would appear that the Republic had more effective slingers than the Empire. The usual range of weights is between 0.7 to 1.75 ounces (Korfmann, 1973: 38). Romans of 40 BCE used a lead projectile that measured 2 inches on its long axis and weighed 1.4 to 2.1 ounces (Mahr, 1964: 120). Maximum weight has been estimated at between 11.5 to 15.7 ounces (Korfmann, 1973: 39). Lead sling projectiles similar to the Roman glandes were used frequently even in the Middle Ages in northern Italy and Germany (Demmin, 1893: 876).

TABLE I: Typical Sling Projectile Weights Compared to a Baseball

											Baseball
Grams	10	20	30	40	50	60	70	80	90	100	142
Grains	154	308	463	616	772	924	1081	1232	1390	1545	2185
Ounces	.35	.70	1.0	1.4	1.76	2.1	2.47	2.8	3.1	3.5	5.0

Velocity and Terminal Effect or Impact

There are a lot of questions yet to be answered about the dynamics of a sling projectile in flight, so that the following is only a very crude analysis of external and terminal ballistics. To determine the theoretical effect of a thrown sling stone, we must have some idea of its velocity on impact.

It has been shown that, for the same impact energy, a heavy projectile traveling slowly does more damage to a living target than a light projectile traveling rapidly (Taylor, 1977: 12–14; O'Conner, 1949: 309). It takes an impact energy of about 70 footpounds* to cause a fracture of most bones of the human body, but less than 2 footpounds to pierce the human body (Gabriel & Metz, 1991: 61). A 2-ounce projectile traveling at 200 feet per second will have an impact energy of 82 footpounds. It is generally agreed that on impact, sling stones could easily penetrate the body of an unarmored man. Biconical sling stones were deadlier than arrows against leather armor (Lindholm, 1940: 7; Mahr, 1964: 123; Korfmann, 1972: 15; Korfmann, 1973: 40), and could cause lethal injury even if they failed to penetrate the armor.

footpound = unit of energy equal to the work done by a force of one pound when its point of application moves through a distance of one foot in the direction of the force.

Hatcher discovered that momentum was a far better indicator of the terminal effect of a projectile than kinetic energy (Josserand & Stevenson, 1972: 148–159). He found that if he combined it with the cross-sectional area of the projectile and a shape factor, he arrived at a formula for relative stopping power (RSP), which was an excellent predictor of comparative impact effectiveness. Using momentum instead of kinetic energy increases the relative significance of the weight of the projectile, which increases the effectiveness of sling stones relative to modern bullets. When we multiply by the cross-sectional areas, which are larger for sling projectiles than for bullets, we increase that relative effectiveness by at least 2 to 4 times. Initially we will neglect the shape factor in our calculations, while recognizing that it too will act to increase the relative effectiveness of sling missiles by an additional small amount, possibly by as much as 25 percent.

From the physical point of view, there are three forces acting on the stone that determine its velocity on impact: the force of the throw, the force of gravity, and the force of drag (air resistance). The force of the throw is applied to the stone only while it is within the sling; and for maximum range, the stone must leave the sling as the sling attains its greatest velocity. Once the stone leaves the sling, gravity and drag are the only forces on the stone, both acting to decelerate it. The initial force on the stone is a function of the speed of the sling at the moment the stone departs it; the force applied by gravity is constant for all practical purposes; but the force of drag is far more complex and far more important than gravity. The stone's inertia, size, shape, and roughness are also important. The stone's inertia determines its resistance to the forces retarding its motion, i.e.

gravity and drag, while the other features determine the effectiveness of drag.

To attempt to calculate drag forces on a sling projectile, even idealized, would be extraordinarily difficult (McDonald, 1960: 463–465; Hatcher, 1962: 549–589), not least because the drag force constantly varies with the velocity of the projectile. As our only purpose is to demonstrate the effectiveness of the ancient sling as a weapon, we will take a simpler approach. Although it is difficult to economically measure the initial or departure velocity of a sling projectile, and the measurement or calculation of drag is extremely difficult, it should be relatively easy to use published values in simple calculations to obtain useful estimates of possible impact velocities and momentum. We will use these estimates to examine two very different tactical situations: (1) high trajectory "plunging" fire and (2) low trajectory "flat" direct fire.

IDEALIZED TRAJECTORY OF A SLING PROJECTILE

This illustration shows the main forces acting on a sling projectile at three significant points on its trajectory. The initial impetus is given by the force of the throw and the inertia (mass) of the projectile maintains the forward and upward motion.

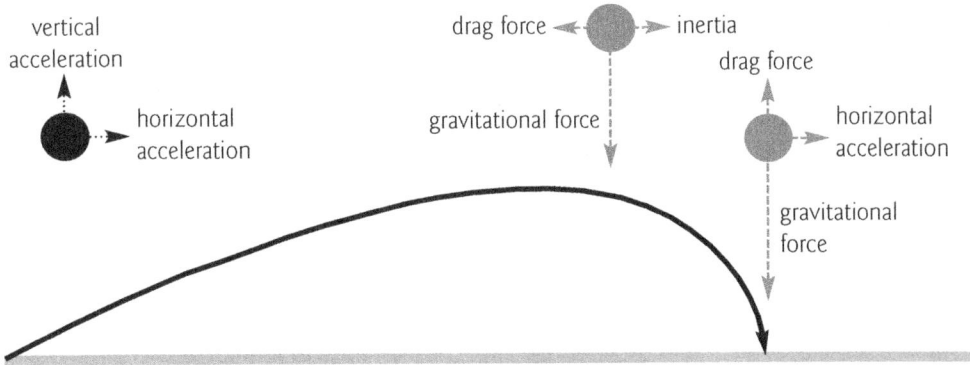

Plunging Fire

In this situation, the projectile is accelerated at a high angle, describing a trajectory of the shape shown. At the trajectory's peak, the two retarding forces have greatly reduced the velocity's horizontal component and the vertical component is zero. That is, the projectile is at rest from the point of view of vertical velocity. Then it starts to fall, and its velocity at impact is now almost exclusively determined by the forces of gravity and drag and the distance it has to fall, gravity acting to accelerate the stone and drag to retard it. When the two forces balance, the stone reaches its terminal velocity. Although a falling sling projectile will never reach more than a fraction of its terminal velocity in any real situation, there are practical situations in which it can reach a substantial fraction of that velocity and the velocities and terminal impact of plunging fire may far exceed that of direct fire with the sling.

As we examine plunging fire, we will look at two effects, the slope of the land and the weight of the projectile. Assuming a maximum range of 330 yards, and a maximum height of 127 yards, we get the following estimated impact velocities and energies and momentum for a 2 ounce projectile thrown out above four different slopes (as our purpose here is to examine the effect of slope only, I have neglected the complexities of air resistance for these first few seconds of fall):

TABLE II: Slope Effect on Impact

Slope	Terminal Velocity	Impact Kenetic Energy	Impact Momentum	Relative Increase in Impact Momentum
0° (level ground)	128 ft/sec*	30 footpound	0.52 lb/sec	1.00
10°	192 ft/sec	75 footpound	0.78 lb/sec	1.50
30°	224 ft/sec	130 footpound	0.91 lb/sec	1.75
45° (100%)	288 ft/sec	170 footpound	1.18 lb/sec	2.27

* ft/sec = feet per second

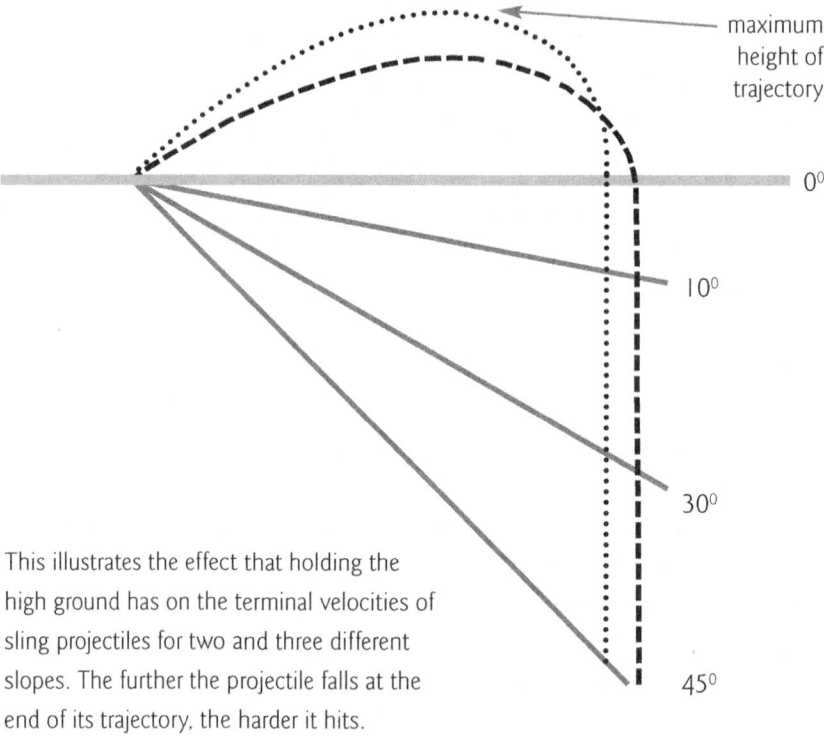

This illustrates the effect that holding the high ground has on the terminal velocities of sling projectiles for two and three different slopes. The further the projectile falls at the end of its trajectory, the harder it hits.

Assuming an impact velocity of 192 feet per second, we may make an initial appraisal of the effect of increasing the weight of sling projectiles on their effectiveness. The different units were selected as we are comparing projectile weights to literature values in grams and to impact energies and momentum from firearms ballistics data published in the United States in British Engineering Units. These differences in units will not affect the validity of our conclusions, as we are only interested in comparative values.

TABLE III

Weight at Impact (grams)	Kenetic Energy at impact (footpounds)	Momentum at impact (lb / sec)	Relative Stopping Power (no units)
50	60	0.66	1.32
100	130	1.32	3.30
200	250	2.64	7.92
300	380	3.951	13.82
400	510	5.28	—
450	570	5.93	—

Cartridge			
32 ACP*	00-129	0.25-0.28	—
.38 Special	260 (military load)	0.55-0.53	0.41
.357 Magnum	535-583	0.87-0.81	0.63
.44 Magnum	971	1.45	1.50
.45 ACP**	356-405 (full metal jacket)	0.88-0.85	0.94-0.90
.223 (Mil)	1290	0.80	—
7.62x39 Soviet***	1527	1.30	0.58

* ACP = automatic centerfire pistol
** .45 ACP = round for the Colt 1911
*** round for the AK47 rifle.

From the table above it is obvious that even lighter sling projectiles have momentum equivalent to modern revolver bullets, and the momentum of heavier sling projectiles exceed those of the two most common military rifle cartridges in use today. In terms of relative stopping power, they are a great deal more effective. Based on these comparisons of momentum, even the 1.75 ounce projectile would be extremely effective on impact. We conclude that the heaviest projectile that a slinger could propel to a useful height was the best to use for plunging fire, and that the heaviest projectiles used could far exceed the terminal effect of modern military small arms.

Direct Fire

When a projectile is thrown directly at a target, gravity and drag act only to reduce the terminal effect of the stone at impact, so terminal effect is strictly a function of the initial velocity imparted to the stone, its density, size, shape, and roughness, and the range to target. We will ignore most of these factors in the analysis that follows, but the reader should remember that they are determinant.

As the weight of the projectile increases, its momentum at departure increases up to the point where the weight starts to reduce the rotational speed of the sling at the instant of release. For a while, the effect will be compensatory, but eventually there will be a net decrease in momentum. This means that the range of weights giving maximum momentum should correspond to the range of most commonly observed weights for sling projectiles discovered in archeological investigations.

To examine the effect of low trajectory, direct fire sling projectiles, we need to have some idea of the initial velocity imparted to such projectile at the instant it leaves the sling, along with an estimate of the average rate at which it loses that velocity while traveling to an estimated maximum range of 109 yards.

Gabriel and Metz state that their experiments (poorly described and admittedly, the efforts of minimally trained slingers) show that the maximum initial velocity obtainable by a sling pouch attached to a 2.5 foot sling was 120 feet per second (1991: 75). But here we have a problem. A major league baseball pitcher can launch a 5 ounce (2,187 grain or 142 gram) baseball at 100 mph or 146 feet per second, unaided by a sling. This would indicate that the values estimated by Gabriel and Metz are far too low to be of any value. So initially, we will assume a velocity at departure of at least 150 feet per second (maximum 200 feet per second), and a percentage loss in velocity of 15 percent over the 109 yards range. For the impact of a 2 ounce projectile, these values give us an impact velocity of 127 feet per second, (maximum 170 feet per second) and an impact momentum of 0.52 lbsec (maximum of 0.72 lbsec), which is about that of a .38 Special revolver.

* lbsec (poundsecond) = An English engineering unit for momentum.

Our baseball figures above lead us to suspect that a substantially heavier missile could be thrown without forcing us to significantly lower our velocity figures. This would of course increase the terminal effect of the sling projectile. We have to assume that a sling projectile could hit at any attitude, but an estimate of the average impact area as nearly one square inch is probably not too far off. So if we include this reasonable estimate of the cross section, we can multiply our impact momentum by a relative factor which gives us an impact effectiveness (relative stopping power = 1.02), which exceeds that of a .357 Magnum at the muzzle. No wonder the sling in skilled hands was such a fearsome weapon. Goliath had just as much chance against David as any Bronze Age warrior with a sword would have had against an adolescent armed with a .45 automatic pistol.

Accuracy

Gabriel and Metz state that even minimal accuracy (no standard given) results in a reduction of velocity by as much as 15 percent. Remembering that training and experience count for a lot with a weapon like the sling and that Gabriel and Metz have been found wanting, we nevertheless can show that velocity of departure has an important effect on accuracy, and that the slinger's timing and release are critical to get a straight cast from the sling to the target.

As a first approximation, we may say that the projectile leaves the sling at a tangent to the arc of a circle for all three throwing styles. What is the angular velocity of the sling at that instant? Assuming the low departure velocity reported by Gabriel and Metz of 120 feet per second and an effective radius of 3 feet for the circular arc followed the sling at release, the sling rotates about 6 times per second. So it only takes 0.02 second to make a 30° difference in the angle of departure. If we use more realistic figures for departure velocity, it takes even less time for significant changes in departure angle to occur, and the probability increases that shots will be off target.

This means that if the sling is whirling horizontally, all other things being equal, this short time available for precise aim will cause lateral deviation from your line of aim. You may adjust elevation by changing the angle of the plane of the circle described by the sling. As the whipping style ends in a horizontal arc, these remarks apply to that style as well. If the sling is whirling vertically, it is easier to control lateral deviation, but it will be harder to correct for elevation.

Hubrecht says that modern slingers reliably hit a target slightly larger than one square yard at a distance of more than 220 yards in the Balearic Isles, but his statement seems to be based on hearsay, rather than direct observation (1964: 93). His exact words are: "On inquiry, I learned that a trained slinger could hit an object a square meter [approx. 1 yard] in size at a distance of 200 meters [220 yards]"; so we must take this claim with a grain of salt. Range estimates by untrained men are notoriously unreliable. Demmin's assertion that primitive peoples armed with the sling were able to resist 19th century soldiers armed with firearms (see below) would seem to indicate that considerable accuracy was possible (1893: 876). Echols states that the Irish used slings up to modern times for war and then for sport, and that a good Irish slinger could hit a shilling as far away as he could see it (1950: 228). Illustrations dating from the Middle Ages show slingers casting single missiles at birds in flight. Throwing at such targets would indicate that a high order of accuracy was possible.

The anecdotal evidence is compelling that the sling can be used with impressive accuracy. However, sling techniques must be practiced until instinctive. There is no time to consciously judge your point of release. Some people will learn to use a sling accurately with relative ease, most will require a lot of practice. The sling is a difficult weapon to learn to use properly.

Three angles of departure 30 degrees apart, resulting from difference of 0.02 seconds in the time of release. One projectile thrown early, one thrown late, and one on target. A high degree of accuracy requires a high level of skill.

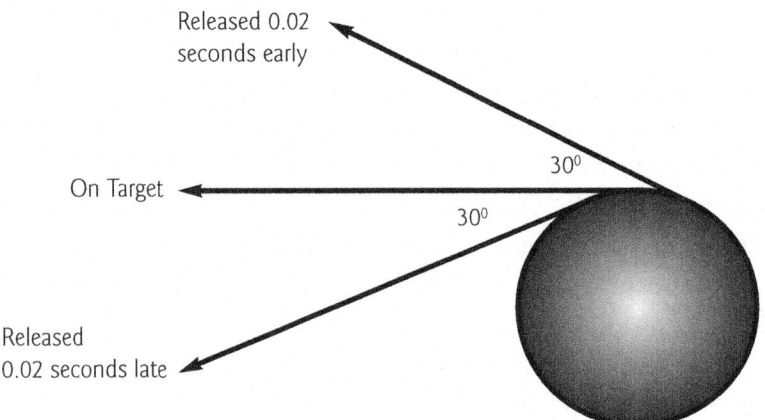

Range

A variety of estimates have been given of the effective range attainable with a sling. Gabriel and Metz state that ancient slingers were only able to *lob* (italics mine) missiles into enemy formations at distances not exceeding 200 yards, and that these had nuisance value at best (1991: 75). However, they also state that small shot (size not given) could be thrown for up to 75 yards with an almost flat trajectory, surely velocities indicative of a very useful extreme range for higher angled fire. Ferrill estimates range at 220 yards or more (1985: 25). The Romans trained at targets (*scopae*) at 200 yards (Watson, 1969: 60). Nineteenth century Tibetans are said to have been able to sling stones to distances exceeding 300 yards (Lindblom, citing Hooker, 1940: 34).

Xenophon says that his slingers out-ranged Persian archers, possibly a range of 330 yards (1959: 81). Connolly estimates sling range as in excess of 380 yards (1981: 49). Demmin mentions "slings, whose range often exceeds 500 paces," and he goes on to say that "Wild people have retained them, and some of them can, with their help, even manage to withstand the fire of carbines" (1893: 876). In expert hands, Hogg estimates this range to be at about 500 yards under ideal conditions (1968: 30). Reid says that he cast a 9-ounce stone ball 60 yards, and 3- and 4-ounce balls to 100 yards (1976: 21). This for an untrained man using a "crude modern sling." Korfmann describes actual observation of untrained slingers reaching a distance in excess of 250 yards using "pebbles selected at random," and he estimates maximum range as 436 yards (1973: 37). The author, an untrained but enthusiastic slinger, has easily thrown beach stones past targets at a known distance of 200 yards.

Gabriel and Metz represent one extreme opinion (but they are not very reliable on slings), while Hogg represents the other. Korfmann is probably the most dependable source, but to be conservative, a tentative value of 380 yards will be taken here to represent the maximum effective range of a sling projectile.

Rate of Fire

Range and rate of fire were important not only from a military point of view, but also for the protection of livestock. Modern man assumes that the shepherd of southern Europe and the Middle East had to contend mainly with wolves, but the lion (*Panthera leo*) was common in North Africa and the Middle East right up to the end of the 19th century. In the second millennium BCE, the lion's range extended into southern Europe (mainly the Balkan Peninsula), Anatolia, and possibly into southern Ukraine. Earlier fossil remains of lions have been found as far north as Poland.

A lion is a much more robust animal than a wolf, and much harder to kill, and like the wolf, the lion is a co-operative hunter. The problem with lions was how to drive them away from your flock without causing a charge. A lion can cover 100 yards from a standing start in 4 seconds, so provoking a charge meant a rapid demotion from shepherd to cat food. So a long-range weapon to shower lions with stones must have seemed useful. I wonder how often it worked. Certainly there was considerable incentive to become proficient and throw a lot of stones as fast as possible from as far away as possible.

Experiments indicate that a sustainable rate of fire of one shot per 10 seconds is a reasonable value for an inexperienced slinger. An experienced slinger could undoubtedly add a few more shots per minute to that rate. We will conservatively assume a maximum sustainable rate of fire to be seven shots per minute.

Relative Effectiveness

The Index of Relative Theoretical Lethality (IRTL) as developed by Dupuy (1985: 27) was used to assess the effectiveness of the sling as a military weapon relative to the other weapons commonly used before the 19th century. The formula reflects the modern military theorist's preoccupation with firepower, and is less sensitive to accuracy, and least sensitive to changes in effective range.

IRTL = $R \times T \times E \times rf \times A \times r$

- R = rate of fire: strike/hour (0.5 rate per minute x 60) = 210
  (maximum sustainable rate 7 per minute x 60 = 420)
- T = targets/strike (relative accuracy) (assume 0.5 average for all ranges)
- E = relative effectiveness (assume armored [0.5] vs. unarmored [0.9] target)
- rf = range factor (1 + [.001 x effective range (meters)]
- A = accuracy (1 sq. yd @ 180 yrds; depends on experience, training, etc.) = 1.0
- r = reliability (assume 1.0)

TABLE IV – Theoretical Lethality Index for the Sling

R	T	Range	rf	Unarmored Target	Armored Target
120	0.5	400	1.63	88.0	48.8
180	0.5	300	1.55	125.4	69.6
180	0.5	350	1.59	128.6	71.4
180	0.5	400	1.63	132.0	73.2
210	0.5	350	1.59	150.3	83.4 (best estimate)
300	0.5	300	1.55	209.2	116.2
420	0.5	350	1.59	300.5	166.9 (max. estimate)

TABLE V – Comparative Index of Relative Theoretical Lethality*

Weapon	IRTL	Ratios**	
Mauser rifle	600	4.00	
Sling	300	2.00	maximum estimate
Handbow	225	1.50	
Sling	150	1.00	best estimate
Crossbow	70	0.47	
Flintlock musket	40	0.26	
Javelin	36	0.24	
Hand-to-hand	32	0.21	
Flintlock rifle	27	0.18	
Matchlock	19	0.13	

* IRTL = Index of Relative Theoretical Lethality (or TLI = Theoretical Lethality Index), an empirical number used for comparing the combat effectiveness of various weapons, devised by the late Colonel R.E. Dupuy.

** IRTL of weapon relative to best estimate of IRTL for sling.

Although tentative, the calculations in Tables IV & V indicate that the sling was a very effective weapon when compared to the other weapons available to ancient or medieval warriors. The sling would appear to have been about two-thirds as effective as a hand bow, and these two weapons were far superior to anything else available in this regard up to the 19th century. In combination with the ballistic information, it justifies the conclusions that the sling was a formidable addition to the armory of any ancient/ medieval army, and that it would have been well while developing tactics allowing its most effective use in the field.

Tactical Considerations

This kind of analysis was unavailable to classical and medieval slingers and their commanders. However, they knew their weapons' limits, characteristics, and performance even if they could not then have known the physical principles underlying that performance. All other things being equal (they never are), our hypothetical slinger wants to produce an impact effect as high as possible. This means that he should select sling, projectiles, and his tactical situation accordingly. When we look at ancient and medieval battles, we find that this is exactly what he did.

The sling has certain advantages over the bow. The sling is useful in any terrain, and an expert can use it with one hand. This means that a slinger can throw while carrying a shield; but an archer cannot shoot while so encumbered. The sling was the weapon of choice for indirect fire on a fortified position (Yadim, 1963: 297) and slingers often began a battle at extreme range, using indirect fire. The sling is less sensitive than a bow to weather influences. Ammunition is almost always available. The sling has the minor disadvantage that it is impossible to use within or from thick vegetation. It is not a practical weapon for forest fighting. Until relatively modern times, however, fighting was generally avoided in forests or heavy cover.

Mahr (1964: 124) makes an observation that tends to clarify a great deal of conflicting data concerning the employment of slingers. It is simply that there were two very different kinds of slingers. The first was the specialist slinger, trained to the weapon from childhood and capable of great accuracy and force (velocity). The sling had other purposes than strictly military and hunting uses, and these other uses provided the training that the best slingers received while still very young. These non-military uses kept the sling alive in more primitive areas of the world right through the period of contact with firearms (Lindblom, 1940: 5). To this day, the sling is still used in some areas for hunting, herding, individual protection, etc. (Lindblom, 1940: 5–25).

The Balearic and Rhodian slingers were excellent examples of this type of specialist slinger brought up with their weapon, and they were used in the role of sharp shooters or snipers. There were never very many of these specialists available relative to other types of soldiers, but they made far better use of the sling than any other troops. Specialist slingers could either be organic to larger formations, or brigaded separately.

The second type of slinger was the relatively untrained peasant, or urban worker. Armed with the inexpensive sling, these low status soldiers were given limited training and were used to produce mass fire at the beginnings of battles. Their hail of sling stones at extreme range produced an effect similar to that of the beaten zone of a modern machine gun, if of much lower lethality. The Romans also attempted to develop this skill as an additional arm for normal infantry (Watson, 1969: 51), but it would seem that these efforts met with indifferent success. The trained legionnaire was more valuable as heavy infantry than light artillery and not sufficiently well trained as a slinger to take up a sniper's role. Davies mentions the sling as a Roman cavalry weapon (1989: 142).

A good tactician will position slingers to get the maximum fall possible on any given battlefield, so it was of great advantage to a commander to position his slingers as high above the enemy as possible. Even a 10-degree slope doubled the impact energy of the falling stones, and more importantly, those projectiles could be a hazard that horses would not face. If properly sited slingers could eliminate the dangers of a cavalry charge across an ancient battlefield, they earned their pay.

Taking the high ground ensured maximum effective (slant) range, and it kept the slingers out of range of "counter-battery" fire. The increased slant range meant that the slingers could bombard their opponents at maximum range, break up tight formations, and enormously increase the fatigue of enemy offensive movement. This was a critical consideration in the days when combat effectiveness depended upon physical strength and speed, and is still tactically important today.

The sling was also a naval weapon, being used from small fighting tops in Egyptian galleys (Yadim, 1963: 252). Once again, we see that slingers were placed as high as possible above the fighting.

There is some confusion concerning the deployment of slingers in battle. Slingers were stationed close to archery units, when present, and were usually stationed behind the archers, one indication that slings had greater range. Gabriel and Metz state that slingers had to be "deployed in mass" to be effective (1991: 75), but Ferrill states that slingers were stationed further apart than archers and did not form a compact line (1985: 25). Trajan's column shows slingers in compact formation with short slings. The amount of space required per slinger depends to a great extent on the length of his sling. With a three-foot sling, there would have to be a minimum distance of nine feet between each slinger to avoid fouling each other's sling or injuring another slinger. Untrained slingers would have to take a relatively open formation, probably a straight line deployed in front of the heavy infantry. An untrained slinger would be a hazard to himself and everyone around him in a dense, compact formation. Even specialist slingers would have to keep an open formation just to have enough room to swing their slings safely. Balearic slingers carried three lengths of sling (Korfmann, 1972: 13) and apparently used the length most suitable for the distance that they had to throw. If specialist troops were delivering high angle, indirect fire, they may have been deployed in several lines.

Gabriel and Metz also state that slinger formations were normally smaller than other combat formations, and were used mostly at the beginning of a battle (1991: 75). I think that this timing would be obvious, since once close-quarter combat was joined, it would be very difficult to select and hit the proper targets. In a defensive role, slingers would open the battle at their extreme range; keeping up fire until the enemy came close enough to be dangerous; then they would retire, either off to the sides, or through the ranks of the heavy infantry. Slingers were generally unarmored and would be extremely vulnerable at close quarters. This is the slinger used as light artillery, a role that they often took at the beginning of a battle.

In an offensive role, specialist slingers would be used as light-infantry skirmishers and snipers, screening movement and concentrating fire on enemy officers, horses, and missile troops. In this role, they could only be used where vegetation or rough terrain gave them protection from cavalry. They could also be used to deliver opening barrages on the assault target, continuing their fire on that target from behind the advancing heavy infantry. Once battle had been joined, they could direct their fire on enemy reinforcements and on the missile troops supporting the enemy heavy infantry. According to Caesar, slingers were also used to repel enemy elephants that would not willingly face showers of sling stones (1976: 226).

Archers and slingers must expose themselves to use their weapons effectively. A first priority in any battle would be to eliminate enemy firepower. So, to use his sling effectively, he had to either be out or range enemy slingers and archers or be shielded from them. If trapped and abandoned by their own heavy troops, as happened in Pompey's army during the Roman Civil War (Caesar, 1976: 153), slingers and archers were defenseless against regular infantry and were often massacred. A slinger depended upon height, distance, movement, cover, or his own heavy troops for his protection. He could generally outrun heavy infantry, but not cavalry. In rough terrain, however, or under the protection of heavy infantry, he was safe from horse troops. Foot or horse caught in rough terrain by slingers occupying high ground were in for a rough time.

Analysis of sling throwing is not enough to bring true skills and understanding of this ancient weapon. Here Dr. Robert Dohrenwend practices various techniques in the wide open spaces in his back yard.

Conclusions

The sling has always been an extremely effective weapon. It is a long range, hard-hitting, accurate weapon with a variety of tactical and civilian uses. It is very light weight, unobtrusive, inexpensive, and its ammunition is easy to obtain and generally free. It is also silent and the ultimate concealable weapon. Its only disadvantage would seem to be the very long period of training and practice required to become acceptably proficient.

The sling has always been a difficult weapon. It has so many obvious advantages over other projectile weapons that it would be difficult to account for its extreme lack of popularity today were it not for the long period of practice necessary to attain proficiency. It can also be a dangerous weapon for the beginner and his surroundings, requiring extensive open ground for safe practice. This requirement is another significant obstacle to a resurgence in its popularity.

The relative isolation of the tribal peoples using slings at the periphery of Asian civilizations may account in large part for the neglect of this weapon by martial artists and martial arts historians. Requiring immense practice to attain proficiency, the hierarchies of these civilizations would rather see their peasant/slave/serf classes at "productive" work than acquiring weapons skills that might lead to a deplorable independence. A formidable and inexpensive personal weapon, absolute governments would rather not see the sling in common use.

These factors may have acted to restrict the sling to the margins of major Asian societies and would help account for the almost complete absence of any discussion of the sling in descriptions of Asian martial traditions. This does not mean that the weapon wasn't there nor that it wasn't used, but rather that we have a major gap in our knowledge of the Asian fighting arts. The weapon has been badly neglected by the modern historian, and today offers an attractive subject for research.

Bibliography

Anderson, J. (1985). *Hunting in the ancient world*. Berkeley: University of California Press.
Blackmore, H. (1971). *Hunting weapons*. New York: Walker.
Blaine, J. (1960). *Rick Brant's science projects*. New York: Grossett & Dunlap.
Caesar, J. (1976). *The civil war*. (J. Gardner, Trans.). New York: Penguin.
Child, V. (1951). *The significance of the sling for Greek prehistory*. Studies presented to David M. Robertson. St Louis.

Connolly, P. (1981). *Greece and Rome at war*. Englewood Cliffs, NJ: Prentice Hall.

Davies, R. (1989). *Service in the Roman army*. New York: Columbia University Press.

De Hoffmayer, A. (1982). *Arms and armour in Spain. Gladius v. II Madrid*. Instituto de Estudios Sobre Armas Antiguas.

Demmin, A. (1893). *Die kriegswaffen in ihren geschichtlichen entwicklelungen von den Ältesten zeiten bis auf die Gegenwart*. Leipzig: P. Friesenhahn.

Dupuy, T. (1985.) *Numbers, predictions & war*. Fairfax, VA: Hero Books.

Echols, E. (1950). The ancient sling. *The Classic Weekly, 18*(15).

Ferrill, A. (1985). *The origins of war*. London: Thames and Hudson.

Friedrici, G. (1910). Verbreitung des Steinschleuder in Amerika. *Z. S. Globus, 98*(17). Braunschweig.

Froissart, J. (1901). *Chronicles, vol. 1*. (T. Johnes, Trans.). London: Colonial Press.

Gabriel, R. & Metz, K. (1991). *From Sumer to Rome: The military capabilities of ancient armies*. Westport, CT: Greenwood.

Hatcher, J. (1935). *Textbook of pistols and revolvers—Their ammunition, ballistics and use*. Plantersville, SC: Small Arms Technical Publishing.

Hatcher, J. (1962). *Hatcher's notebook*. (3rd ed.) Harrisburg, PA: Telegraph Press.

Hawkins, W. (1847). Observations on the use of the sling. *Archeologica, 32*.

Hogg, O. (1968). *Clubs to cannon: Warfare and weapons before the introduction of gunpowder*. London: Gerald Duckworth & Co.

Hubrecht, A. (1964). The use of the sling in the Balearic Isles. *Bulletin van de Vereenignig tot Bevordering der Kennis van de Antseke Beschouing, 39*.

Josserand, M. & Stevenson, J. (1972). *Pistols, revolvers, and ammunition*. New York: Bonanza.

Korfmann, M. (1972). Schleuder und Bogen in Sudwestasien von den frühsten Belegen bis zum Begin der historisches Stadtstaaten. *Antiquitas 3*, Band 13. Bonn.

Korfmann, M. (1973, October). The sling as a weapon. *The Scientific American, 299*(4).

Lindblom, K. (1940). The sling, especially in Africa. *Smärre Meddalanden, 17*. A report published by The Ethnographic Museum of Sweden.

Mahr, H. (1964). Die Steinschleuder, eine der ältesten Waffen der Menscheit. *Waffen und Kostümkunde* (2).

McDonald, J. (1960). An aid to computation of terminal fall velocities. *Journal of Meteorology, 17*, 463–465.

O'Conner, J. (1949). *The rifle book*. New York: Knopf.

Reid, W. (1976). *Arms through the ages*. New York: Harper and Row.

Savage, C. (1984). *The sling for sport and survival*. Port Townsend, WA:

Loompanics.
Taylor, J. (1977). *African rifles and cartridges*. Highland Park, NJ: The Gun Room Press.
Warry, J. (1980). *Warfare in the classical world*. New York: St. Martins.
Watson, G. (1969). *The Roman soldier*. Ithaca: Cornell University Press.
Xenophon. (1959). *The anabasis: The march up country*. (W. Rouse, Trans.). New York: Mentor.
Yadim, Y. (1963). *The art of warfare in Biblical lands in the light of archeological discovery*. London: Weidenfield and Nicholson.

The Odd East Asian Sai

Introduction

    I doubt that anyone really believes the old story of Okinawan weapons originating as peasant farm tools. Their real origins are more plausible and far more interesting, and the following story of the origin and development of the Okinawan sai seems to best fit the published evidence so far available in English.

    It is likely that the sai developed from a very old weapon, the trident spear, which may have originated in India or Indonesia, and which was distributed throughout East Asia in antiquity. The sai originated either when the three-pronged head from a broken trident spear was grabbed and used defensively in combat, or when that spearhead was deliberately dismounted from its shaft and developed into a close-quarter defensive weapon. There is also enough circumstantial evidence to force us to seriously examine the possibility that the example of the European left hand dagger may have strongly influenced or inspired this latter development.

    Metals and their ores are very scarce on Okinawa, so it is virtually a certainty that any metal weapons found there were imported. Instructional lineages and katas for the sai make their first appearance in Okinawan history in the late 17th century, and tradition suggests that the sai handle lacked a pommel and was pointed (Sakagami, 1974: 14; Matayoshi, 1995b). Such a handle makes sense only as the tang of a spearhead. So, it is likely that spearheads for the trident spear were deliberately imported into Okinawa from China before 1699 for use as sais.

The Okinawans probably completed the conversion of those spearheads to the sai, giving it the configuration we know today. Although 18th and 19th century examples of the sai may be found from China (Richard Florence, personal communication), there is nothing to show that these examples with rebated points are not based on a weapon which originated in Okinawa. This possibility needs further study. The sai's rebated points and lack of blade made it more acceptable for such justifiable and limited use in the political eyes of the Satsuma officials governing Okinawa. The sai became a regulation weapon for maintaining palace security and public order, and was used by police in the major Okinawan port cities. Even within the police force, it was always the weapon of a small elite. After the Meiji Restoration in Japan in the third quarter of the 19th century, the sai was adopted by civilians in the more general practice of martial arts, gradually attaining wider popularity.

The evidence for these assertions is in five parts: first, the nature of the weapon itself; second, the instructional lineages, known and legendary; third, sai techniques as revealed by the existing katas; fourth, the sai's current and historical distribution in southeast Asia; and finally the geographical, historical, and social conditions in South East Asia, and especially Okinawa, between 1540 and 1879. Now to begin, let's consider the sai.

The Weapon

What is a sai? In English, the word *sai* has been variously translated as "fork," "short sword," "truncheon" (most common), or "trident." None of these English terms are really satisfactory, although trident is probably the best from an historical viewpoint. The weapon is unique and can simply be called a *sai*.

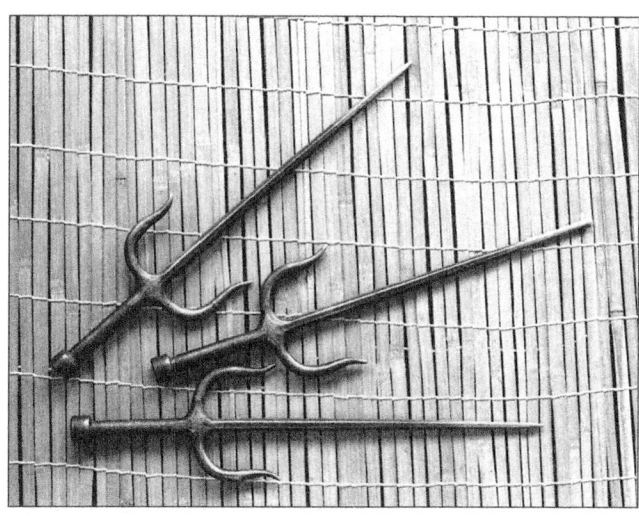

Set of three sais.
Photo courtesy of Mary Bolz.

Usually constructed as a single piece of chrome plated or blued steel, the sai does vaguely resemble a trident. The central shaft is flanked by two prongs or tines, about one-third the length of the shaft. The shaft may be round or octagonal, more rarely hexagonal. The advantage of an octagonal shaft is that it will deal a blow of more concentrated force. The point of the shaft is blunt or rebated; the tines are pointier but also not normally sharpened. The handle is round and is normally wrapped with leather, cord, or similar material to provide a good gripping surface. There is a blunt pommel at the end of the handle. The average weight is about one pound, 10 ounces, but the size of the weapon depends on the size of the person wielding it. The shaft should extend about one inch past the elbow to fully protect the forearm, and when held in the thrust (*tsuki*) position, the tip of the forefinger should touch the base of the pommel.

The blunt points are logical only as a design feature to limit lethal effects. Although the sai can be used to inflict horrific injuries, especially if thrusts with the point of the shaft are directed against soft areas of the body or strikes are directed at the head, the sai is designed to limit these effects and to give the man using it more control over the injuries inflicted by his weapon. The iron material was chosen to minimize shock when blocking other impact weapons and to ward off bladed weapons more effectively.

PARTS OF THE SAI

Most modern instructors believe that originally the point, tines, and pommel of the sai were all sharp. The statement that the pommel was sharp is particularly interesting. In general, spears have only two types of tangs, sockets or spikes.

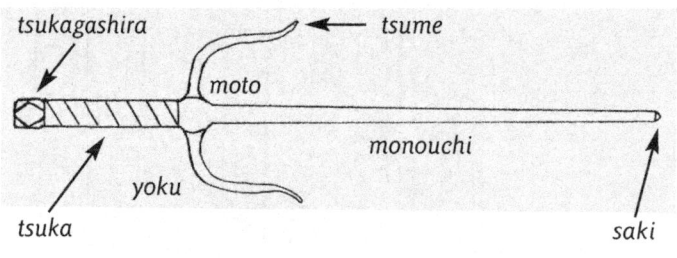

monouchi — shaft, blade
moto — cross block, center of balance
saki — tip, point
tsuka — hilt (handle)
tsukagashira — pommel, butt
tsume — guard tips
yoku — wing, guard, prong, tine

If the first sais originated as the heads of trident spears with spike tangs, they would have long, pointed handles with no pommels. Pointed sais still exist, as do sais with blades instead of round or octagonal shafts. But these weapons are rare, the bladed ones recent, and all that I have seen, have pommels.

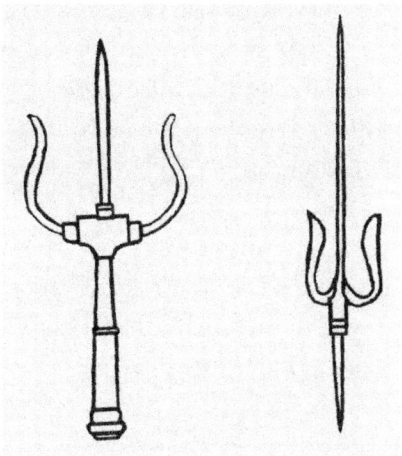

Trident spearheads or rudimentary sais? Note the spiked tang which gives the spearhead on the right a sharp handle. The earliest sais were probably an adaptation of this type of spearhead.

Illustration of a trident spear from Yi Dok-Mu's *Encyclopedia of Illustrated Martial Arts Manual (1790)*.

In the light of the above, we should mention the hypothesis that the sai developed from the head of the *nunte* (later called the *manji-sai*), a combination fish spear/gaff. A fish spear without barbs seems odd, but perhaps it was used as a boat hook. Anyway, McCarthy states that the manji-sai and the kata Jigen no-manji-sai were developed by Taira Shinken (1898–1970) on the basis of both the original nunte and the sai (Shinken, 1999: 106–107). If he is correct, the manji-sai could not have been the precursor to the sai, but the interesting point here is that the long pointed tang used to fasten the head of the manji-sai to the pole to form the nunte is still the handle of the manji-sai. The recent development of the manji-sai from the nunte is an example of the recent use of a dismounted spearhead as a separate weapon.

The manji-sai has to have a shorter shaft than the normal sai, otherwise the manji-sai would become unwieldy. For that reason, the manji-sai is less useful for blocking techniques than the sai. It is hard to believe that it will survive in weapons practice except as an odd curiosity.

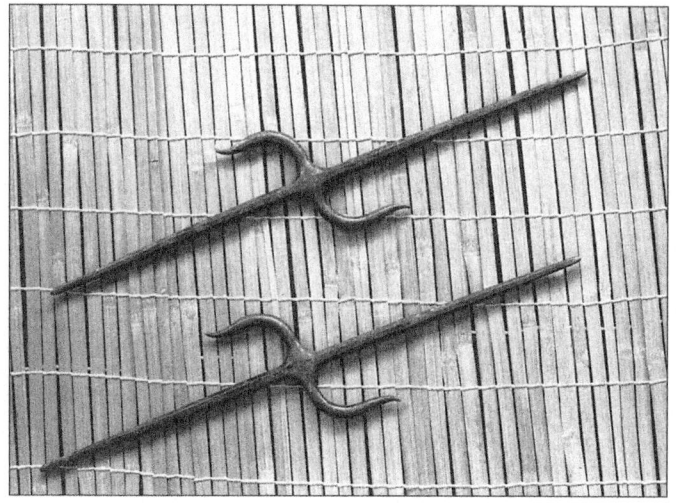

Set of manji-sais. Photo courtesy of Mary Bolz.

The sai is always used in pairs with one in each hand. Some authorities state that sais are supposed to be carried in sets of three, so that two of them can be thrown! Most sources, however, agree that one was to be thrown, and it is hard to believe that two of the three sais were to be thrown as all kata and techniques involve two sais. Throwing a single sai could be used to distract an opponent armed with a long weapon, allowing you to close the range as he dodged to avoid the spinning, heavy sai. A skillful throw might even put your opponent into the exact position required for the technique to subdue him. A really skillful and lucky throw might put him out of action altogether.

The sai was much used in the waterfront areas of Naha and Tomari. Prior to 1870, the Okinawan police carried it... Usually three sais were carried were carried in case one was lost... or thrown.

– Corcoran & Farkas, 1993: 86

A policeman arrives on the scene with sai in hand.
The drawing is from a novel titled *Tales of the Hermit, Vol. 1*,
by O. Ratti & A. Westbrook. © 2001 Futuro Designs & Publications.

The sai is an awkward shape to try to conceal on one's person, and it is heavy. No provision was ever made for a scabbard for the original weapon. The first practical holster for the sai was developed only a few years ago by RRB for their police baton of similar design to the sai.[1] The sai was obviously supposed to be carried openly, and a weapon carried openly is intended as a symbol of armed authority. While more expensive than wooden weapons, the sai was less expensive than any bladed weapon of comparable strength.

These characteristics lead us to the tentative conclusion that the sai was adopted in Okinawa as a weapon for the civil authority, i.e. the police. Only police need non-lethal, issue impact weapons carried openly as symbols of authority.

Most of what has been argued so far can be corroborated in the Japanese language text:

Every country has its own martial arts for the protection of its citizens. However the sai of Ryukyu is unlike the martial arts of other countries in that it is not to stab the opponent to death, but to subdue without mortal injury. This has a meaning so deep that words cannot express. The fact that the Ryukyuan sai took its shape from the human form can also be said to be testament to its use as a peaceful weapon. It is also interesting to note that the old sai have rounded knobs at the tip of the shaft. More recent sai are sharpened at the tip, and one can often see practitioners throwing them through the floor at demonstrations. However, when considering the old sai, the modern ones seem to be headed down the wrong path. The Ufuchiku used the sai, whereas the Chikusaji carried the *bo* [staff].[2] The sai is considered to be a weapon, but practice with the sai can also be used to strengthen the wrists. The fact that it lacks a cutting edge makes it markedly different from other weapons, such as a sword or a spear. Currently, the sai are often used in pairs, but sometimes a third is carried in the sash [*obi*] (as a backup after throwing one). The old police inspectors carried the sai in order to protect the King, control crowds, and arrest criminals. This makes it similar to the jitte of mainland Japan.[3]

Saijutsu Instructors and Lineage in Okinawa

The sai and its techniques first appear on Okinawa almost exclusively among police and those responsible for royal security.[4] Virtually all of the earlier instructors who trained and taught before 1870 were members of the Okinawan aristocracy connected with these activities. All modern instructional lineages are related, and none are independent. When we trace these lineages back in time, they go no further than the late 17th or early 18th centuries, a point at which the lineages become imprecise and even somewhat legendary (see Table I).

According to Taira in his Japanese language text *Ryukyu Kobudo Taikan* (1964), Hamahiga accompanied King Sho Shin and Prince Nago Chogen on their trip to Edo, where he played a game of Go with the famous Japanese master Hon'inbo Dosaku on 17 April, 1682. It is also said that with the permission of Shimazu Hidehisa of Satsuma, Hamahiga also performed karate (*toudi*) and saijutsu in front of the 4th Shogun Tokugawa Tsunayoshi. His sai kata later became known as *Hamahiga no sai*, and is still practiced in Okinawa today. Hamahiga Peichin is believed to have developed the *Hamahiga no sai* and *Hamahiga no tonufa kata* which bear his name. Shitahaku Oyakata (or Uekata) lived during the reign of the Okinawan King Sho Tei (1669–1709) and the kata *Tsuken (Chiken) Shitahaku no sai* may be tentatively attributed to him. These two men would seem to be the earliest known sai instructors in Okinawa (Mario McKenna, personal communication).

TABLE I: Principal Instructional Sai Lineages

Early Sai Masters – Shitahaku, Oyakata (17–18c)
Yara, Chatan (1668–1756, studied in China)

Part One:

Sakugawa, Kanga (1782–c.1862)
|
Chinen, Pechin (??)
|
Chinen, Sanda (1842–1928)
|
├──────────────┬─────────────── Tawada, Shimbuku (1851–1920)
| | |
Chodo, Oshiro   Chinen, Masami   (ukn in Taiwan)
(1887–1935)   (1898–1976)
                |
        ┌───────┴───────┐
        Nakazato, Shugoro   Higa, Seitoku
        (1919–)   (1931–)

Part Two:

Sakugawa, Kanga (1733–c.1815)
|
Matsumora, Soken (Royal Body Guard) (1809–1901)
|
Gushikawa, Tiragwa (1870–1924)
|
Matayoshi, Shinko (1888–1947)
|
Matayoshi, Shinpo (1921–1997)
|
Many instructors world-wide
Goju-Ryu or Pangai-Noon-Ryu
•
•

Part Three:

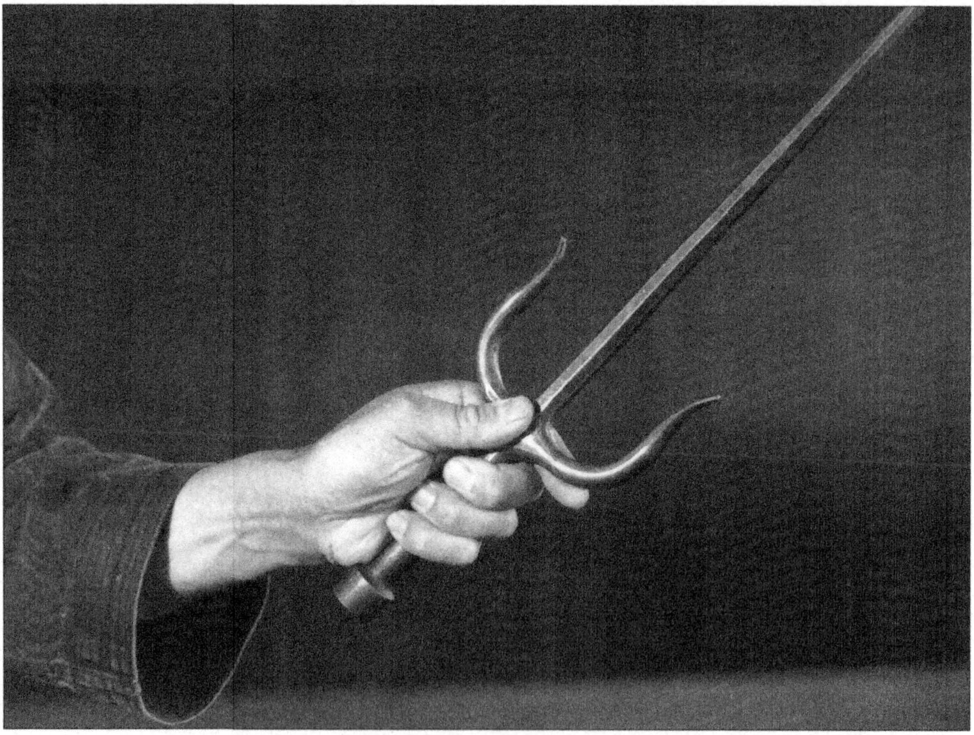

```
                          Higa, Matsu (Royal Bodyguard)
                                 (1790–1870)
                                      |
        Chinen, Sanda          Kanakushiku, Sanda
         (1842–1928)        (1841–1920, 1921 or 1926)
              |                       |
              └──── Yabiku, Moden ────┬──────────────────── Kina, Shosei
                     (1878–1941)      │                      (1882–1981)
                          │           │                           |
                          │           │                       Isa, Kaishu
              ┌───────────┼───────────┤                         (1943–)
        Taira, Shinken              Mabuni, Kenwa
         (1887–1970)                 (1889–1957)
              |                           |
   ┌──────────┼──────────┐           Uechi, Kanei
Akamine, Eiiryo  Inoue, Motokatsu  Sakagami, Ryusho   (1911–1991)
 (1918-1993)     (1915–1993)       (1915–1993)
      |               |                 |
 Shorin-Ryu &    Murakami, Katsumi  Demura, Fumio
 Uechi-Ryu         (1927– )          (1938– )
 instructors
```

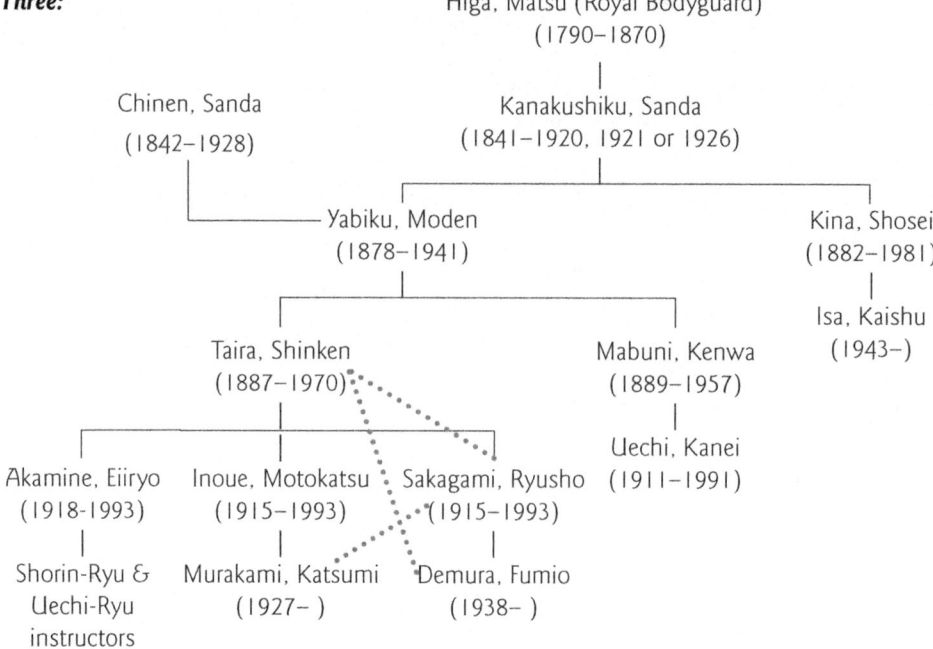

Gripping a sai. Photo courtesy of Mary Bolz.

There is no direct connection known between Shitahaku Oyakata or Hamahiga and the next known instructors, Yara Chatan,[5] "Tode" Sakugawa (1733–1815), and Higa Matsu (1790–1870), but their lives appear to overlap in time. There is a sai kata attributed to Yara Chatan (*Chatan Yara no sai*) and we can begin to trace connected instructional lineages with Sakugawa and Matsu Higa, who was responsible for royal security and was Kankushiku Ufuchiku's instructor.

Kanakushiku (a.k.a. Kanagusuku Sanda) or simply called by his rank, *Ufuchiku*, was a senior Okinawan police official in the mid-19th century, and was central in the adoption of the sai as one of the five major traditional Okinawan weapons.

> ...police commissioner of Shuri, Okinawa, and personal body guard for Shota-O (Sho-Tai), the last reigning King of the Ryuku Islands (1848–1879) . . . and responsible for the king's safety and the security of the castle grounds, . . . passing on a system of kobujutsu which was actually an advanced police science. many of its weapons are believed to have been confiscated and adapted from criminal elements. . . trained two chief disciples: Saburo Takashiki and Shosei Kina.
> – Corcoran & Farkas, 1993: 389

Kankushiku was a highly significant figure in the modern history of the sai, as according to the chart shown, most modern instructors can trace their lineages back through him. But a word of caution is in order. The chart which suggests his importance was developed from admittedly deficient evidence. Taira Shinken and Yabiku Moden are also key figures in sai instruction.

Sai Katas

Katas have been created, modified, and forgotten in Okinawa ever since the development of the fighting arts (*te*) and the introduction of the traditional weapons (*kobudo*). This evolutionary process, which is perfectly normal in Okinawan martial arts,[6] is going on today, and most sai katas are very recent, usually named for the well-known instructors who devised them. However, our main interest here is in the oldest katas, which may be attributed to the later half of the 17th century or first decades of the 18th century. There are none of earlier origin, but it is quite possible that older katas may have been lost.

> It is believed that many kobudo kata have come and gone because of inadequate teaching methods.
> – Taira Shinken

There are at least 23 generally accepted sai katas with status confirmed by their appearance in two or more published sources. As these katas seem to be the best known, it is likely that they will remain central to sai training in the future. In addition, there are at least fourteen other sai katas which have so far been mentioned in only one published source. These katas seem to have a more tenuous position in sai training, but some may be taught at least as widely as the more publicized 23. There are undoubtedly other sai katas which have not been mentioned in print at all, but with 37 known katas, saijutsu has a secure place in Okinawan kobudo (See Table II).

TABLE II: 37 Sai Katas

23 Confirmed Traditional Katas
(two or more published sources; various spellings)

1) Tawada no sai ichi
2) Matsumura no sai
3) Tsuken (Chikin) Shitahaku no sai
4) Hama Higa no sai
5) Chatan Yara no sai
6) Hama Udun Yakaa no sai
   (Yakaa no sai)
7) Hantagawa Kouraguwa no sai
   (Hanta Guwa Kuruguwa sai)
8) Kogosuku no sai
9) Kyan no sai
10) Kishaba no sai – sho
11) Kishaba no sai – dai
12) Ufuchiku no sai

Kuniyoshino sai (Ryuei-ryu sai ni):
13) Sai 1 (aka Kuniyoshi dai ichi)
14) Sai 2 (aka Kuniyoshi dai ni)
15) Sai 3 (aka Kuniyoshi dai san)
16) Matayoshi no sai nicho sai
    (aka Matayoshi no sai ichi)
17) Sancho sai
    (aka Matayoshi no sai ni)
18) Tokuyama no sai (2)
19) Shinbaru no sai
20) Aragaki (Arakaki) no sai
21) Kugushiku no sai (Kojo no sai)
22) Matsu Higa no sai
23) Jigan no manji-sai

14 Unconfirmed Traditional Katas
(Mentioned in only one published source)

1) Higanna no sai (Goju-Ryu lineage)
2) Kojokage
3) Chihara no sai
4) Tokumine no sai
5) Ishiguwa (Ishikawa) no sai
6) Shitahaku no sai
7) Shikawaguwa no sai
8) Ishikawaguwa no sai
9) Nakamura no sai
10) Sakugawa no sai
11) Shimabuku no sai ichi
12) Shimabuku no sai ni
13) Shishiryu no sai (Kudoka no sai)
14) Soken no sai

Saijutsu is not simply karate with a weapon in each hand. Footwork is different; body positioning is different; timing is different; distancing is different; and rhythm is different. Hip rotation is much less important for power generation than in karate. Power in the sai comes from the proper use of hand, wrist and elbow coordination to control the trajectory and speed of the weapon. The weapon is whipped into impact. The configuration of the weapon to a large degree determines the positioning of hand and arm. Sai katas and karate katas generally differ enough in basics to faintly suggest that the sai may have originated in a separate martial tradition.

Still, karate has had a strong and obvious influence on training with the sai,[7] and in Kenshinjan Shorin-Ryu karate, which does not use hip rotation to generate power, the saijutsu is much closer in basics to the karate techniques taught in that style. The embusen of their 3rd-dan sai kata is even based on that of Ananku kata (Richard Florence, personal communication). This is extremely interesting and a detailed comparison of their saijutsu with their karate might make an important contribution to our understanding of both.

Almost all of the sai techniques may be interpreted in terms of blocking, disarming, and subduing an antagonist. Thrusts with the point of the shaft do occur,[8] but most attention in training is paid to flipping the weapon in rapid swinging strikes (*furi*) with the side of the shaft, thrusts with the butt (*tsuki*), and various blocking techniques. The various furi seem to be mostly directed at fingers, wrists, lower arms, and elbows. Such techniques are intended to disarm, intimidate, and apprehend an opponent, not to destroy him. The preponderance of such techniques in the kata confirms the conclusion that the sai was normally used as a police weapon.

Parenthetically, there is a movement in a number of sai katas which seems to make little or no sense at all. The sai is reversed and the weapon is grasped by the tapered shaft and thrust at the opponent, hilt forward, ostensibly to hook the opponent with the tines of the guard. This is a very dangerous and silly move, unless the opponent is already badly hurt and dazed. The hilt could be easily grasped by an opponent, and the tapered shaft only affords a very weak grip. The officer could find himself disarmed and in serious trouble.

Historically, as a police weapon, the sai could not have been developed to face warriors with swords. Police do not normally attack their superiors. Even so, such kata applications as I have seen demonstrated show the sai used against a long weapon, mostly against the staff or the sword. However, it is extremely unlikely that Okinawan saijutsu was ever developed as a defense against Japanese warriors. The use of the sai against a sword is a little like its use against a .44 Magnum. You'd have to be dead lucky, or you'd quickly just be dead.

It is also unlikely that the sai was used very often against other kobudo weapons. Mostly the police were armed in this way, and police do not normally attack each other. It is more probable that the sai was used to counter knives of varying size, clubs, and other such improvised weapons as might occur to drunken or otherwise unruly sailors. The sai was also likely used to counter opponents using traditional Okinawan fighting techniques (*te*), as a strong block will often discourage further attack, even when the blocker is unarmed. A strong block with a sai would probably end any confrontation with an unarmed man immediately. Sai katas should be studied with these more realistic applications in mind.

Distribution and History

Although the sai is especially popular in Okinawa and Indonesia, the weapon is widely used today in the various martial arts found in the countries around the East and South China Seas. It is known as the *tepki* in Malaysia; the *tjabang* (or *cabang*) in Indonesia, and as the *trisula* in India and the Sundanese Islands. It was called the *san-ku-cho*, *titjio* or *titcher* (?) in China, and Draeger shows an Indonesian sai pair also called *titjio* (1972: 82), although titjo would seem to be the name used in southern China. It was also called a *teshaku* (Sells, 1998: 43). There is an Indonesian variant called a *siku-siku* which has one tine turned up and the other turned down similar to the manji-sai, but the siku-siku is still usually mounted on a staff where it becomes the head of a pole arm (*nunte*). The sai is no longer used anywhere in the region as a police weapon.

The sai is not found in the Philippines, either as a police weapon or as a martial arts weapon. And this is very interesting, given the Philippine tendency to use a weapon (bladed or stick) in each hand and the profound influence of Spanish fencing on the development of martial arts there. The sai seems to have spread along the coasts of the East China Sea only where there was an organized indigenous government which required such a weapon for internal security and urban public order. In the Philippines, the Spanish took over the development and control of urban centers and preferred more familiar European weapons for maintaining public order.

Although it is just barely possible that the sai was introduced to Okinawa by the Japanese (Satsuma clan) themselves to replace bladed weapons for Okinawan court security, and possibly even for police use supervised by the Okinawan aristocracy, it does not appear that the sai was ever adopted to any extent as a police or martial arts weapon in either Korea or Japan. However, there is an early Korean trident spearhead with tines identical to those of the sai (Stone, 1961: 629), and the Japanese *jutte* (or *jitte*), a more recent weapon, was used by the police of the Tokugawa Shogunate, possibly taking the sai as its inspiration.

The jutte is not a sai, but a different weapon altogether, and the Korean spearhead would seem to be a copy of a Chinese weapon.

These considerations indicate that the sai, or precursor weapons to the sai, were imported to Okinawa from either Indonesia or China. If from Indonesia, it is most likely that the sai arrived in Okinawa sometime in the late 15th century, if from China, 200 years later. Historical circumstances make it impossible to eliminate either possibility, but the evidence favors the Chinese source.

Indonesia

Donn Draeger (1972: 33) has suggested on the basis of sculptural evidence in Java,[9] that the sai originated in Indonesia as the *tjabang*, or perhaps even India (*trisula*), before the 7th century, and well before it has been found in either China or Okinawa.

> Tjabang: used in Indonesia and Malaysia, originated within the Hindu culture which entered Indonesia around 300–400 AD. ... used in pairs, one in each hand.
> – Corcoran & Farkas, 1993: 157

Mr. Richard Lopez demonstrating Indonesian techniques of the tjabang.

Sakagami (1974: 14) says that the sai may have evolved from a sword held by Buddhist representations of Indra, a major Hindu god adopted by Buddhists as a protective deity. The graceful sweeping curve of the tines of the sai resemble the curves of the horns of the water buffalo. This may have been part of the original tjabang design, as it developed in Indonesia, combining symbolism with practicality.

According to Draeger (1972: 33), the tjabang was a defensive pre-Majapahit (before 1292) weapon, antedating the spread of Islam in Indonesia, and he also stated that there was early contact between western Indonesia and Okinawa. This contact would likely have occurred during the Majapahit period (1292–1480), for this loosely confederated Javanese Empire was enormous, possessing a very widespread trading network and a dominant naval presence in Southeast Asia. To confirm the Indonesian origin of the sai, the ancient statue(s) specifically displaying sais, which Donn Draeger reported seeing in Indonesia,[10] must be located, photographed, described, and their age authenticated and attested. Until that is done, we have no real proof that the sai was present in Indonesia before 1600 or that the weapon originated there.

The distribution of the tjabang in Indonesia today seems to lie largely in those islands most heavily influenced by European colonial powers (Draeger, 1972). Skill with the weapon seems to be especially well developed in the Moluccas. This may argue a European influence, but Indonesian styles adopt freely any technique that works from any foreign style they encounter, and today, almost everywhere in Indonesia the tjabang (sai) is used in pairs as a rebated weapon, just as in Okinawa. Given the Indonesian preference for bladed weapons, it is entirely possible that traditional Okinawan martial arts (te) influenced the development of Indonesian styles, such as pentjak-silat, during the Majapahit period. If the sai originated in Indonesia, then it is possible that the sai was subsequently lost as a police weapon in Indonesia during the period of Dutch colonial rule, and that the modern tjabang and its techniques were re-introduced from Okinawa as a martial arts weapon after WW II.

McCarthy (1999: 125, fn. 34) states that the staff and sai were official police weapons in Okinawa throughout the 16th century. We have seen that there is considerable circumstantial evidence showing that the sai was always a police weapon. If McCarthy and Draeger are correct, the sai may well have come from Indonesia during the Majapahit period (1292–1480), before its adoption as a police weapon in Okinawa. As there was known to be official contact between Okinawa and Indonesia in the 15th and 16th centuries, and as this was an age of great commercial activity centered on Okinawa, the historical timing is good. This theory for the origin of the sai remains plausible and cannot be dismissed on the basis of the available evidence.

However, there is some difficulty in accepting McCarthy's statement concerning the 16th century presence of the sai in Okinawa. We have seen that the lineage and kata evidence goes back only to late 17th or early 18th century, and that mention of the sai disappears there. The older members among the 20th century Okinawan masters seem to remember being told that the sai was originally sharp, with both Matayoshi Shinpo and Sakagami Ryusho stating that the handle lacked a pommel and was also sharp. These statements are very significant, as coming from such influential modern masters, they strongly suggest that the sai came to Okinawa as a dismounted trident spearhead at a very early stage in its development.

Now, if this is remembered today, but neither kata nor instructors (even legendary) go back further than the last quarter of the 17th century, we have weak circumstantial evidence that the sai was introduced to Okinawa at that time, and that it took on its modern form within Okinawa. If the sai had arrived in Okinawa in its present configuration, it had to have come from an indigenous society with sufficient structure to support organized police, i.e. China, Japan, or Korea. But we now have reason, however shaky, to believe that it did not arrive in Okinawa as the fully developed sai.

China

There is no shortage of possible Chinese precursors to the Okinawan sai, and Yang (1999: 34, 52, 78) describes several related Chinese weapons:

1) The *cha* (*san cha* or *san gu cha*). As shown, the tines of these long trident spears, have the curved sweep characteristic of modern sai tines. In southern China, the points of shaft and tines were tapered, and if dismounted from its pole the spearhead would make a good sai.
2) The *bi jia cha*. A favorite White Crane weapon about 20 inches long, this short sword with sai-type quillons makes a good candidate for the sai as it arrived in Okinawa, except that this weapon was bladed.
3) The *duan cha*, an odd short trident. It least resembles the modern sai, with the central shaft almost as long as the side tines and a long handle relative to the rest of the weapon. According to Yang it was used in pairs as a defensive weapon.
4) Yang states categorically that the sai originated as the *chai* (a hairpin!) probably during the Ming Dynasty (1368–1644 AD) and was later a favorite weapon in Guangdong and Fujian provinces. The hairpin in question is known as a *kanzashi* in standard Japanese, and the similarity between its shape and that of the sai has been noted by Nakamoto Masahiro. It is unlikely that this *kanzanshi* was the inspiration for the sai (Mario McKenna, personal communication).

The three trident weapons were popular in southern China and Taiwan. They were originally hunting weapons and were then adapted for use against bandits and other human predators. They must have been well known and readily available to Okinawans visiting China. Sakagami (1974: 11) states that the Chinese weapon, the *san-ku-ch'u* (Yang's *san-gu-cha*), was the forerunner of the Okinawan sai, but this weapon may have entered China from India or Indonesia. Given the strong commercial ties between Okinawa and China in the 15th and 16th centuries, it is more probable that the sai came to Okinawa from China, rather than directly from Indonesia.

There are two possibilities here. First, China, a civilized nation, had established agencies to maintain public order. These agencies might well have originated and adopted the sai as a police weapon, and it was for that use that the fully developed sai was imported to Okinawa. Second, possibly inspired by Portuguese/Spanish rapier and dagger technique, the Okinawans saw the possibilities inherent in the detached trident spearhead as a defensive hand weapon, imported the spear heads to Okinawa and developed the sai there. On balance, the evidence would indicate the san gu cha trident spear as the precursor to the Okinawan sai. As it would seem that the trident spear was more popular on the Asian mainland than in Japan, we may tentatively conclude that the sai first came to Okinawa as spike tang, trident spearheads from its largest trading partner, China.

The sai, unlike the manji-sai, is not longitudinally symmetrical and a pointed handle would quickly become a dangerous annoyance. While the shaft and tines might have retained their points for a considerable period, we might expect that the pointed handle would have been eliminated soon after the spearhead became the hand-held sai. As the importation of spearheads into Okinawa after 1699 is highly unlikely, we may say that these weapons entered Okinawa from China in the last half of the 17th century. And now we have to ask if European influence or inspiration was at all likely at this time.

European Influence in East Asia

The sai was principally used for blocking, so it is a fair question to ask what was used in the other hand for offense. Today we answer, another sai! But, was that always the case? In this regard, attention must be paid to the late medieval and Renaissance European left hand daggers (*poniards*) used in conjunction with rapiers. These daggers were mainly used for blocking, but many offensive techniques were taught as well (Hergsell, 1998: 184–204). The European left-hand dagger was produced in many versions. Some of them had rings, shells, and other components of a complex guard, and normally their edges were sharp all the way to the base of the guard. These features precluded their use as a sai, although a simple ring on the quillon block would not have been a serious obstacle provided that the thumb was placed on the opposite side. Other daggers, narrow bladed, and rigid, however, had ample ricassos and simple cross guards with long quillons bending toward the point of the dagger. Combining such a guard with a relatively long ricasso* permits most sai techniques to be used with a left hand dagger.

* *Ricasso*: that part of a sword or knife blade next to the hilt, quadrangular in cross-section to allow the fingers to rest on this section of the blade without getting cut.

During this period in Europe, there was considerable experimentation with serious fencing and other martial techniques, and the various instructors were both pragmatic and inventive. It would be curious indeed if someone had not independently developed and taught dagger techniques similar to those for the sai. However, the likely European contribution would be the idea of using two weapons simultaneously in each hand, one defensively and one offensively.

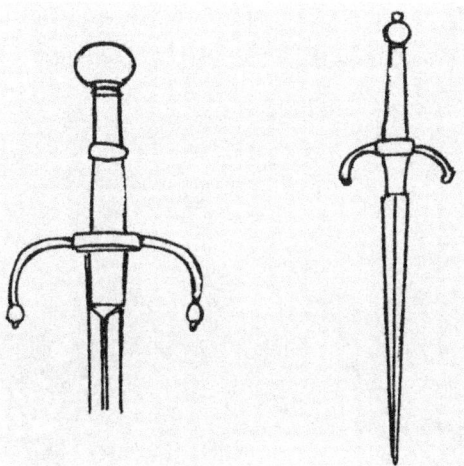

Two European left-hand dagger hilts showing similarities to sai hilts.

The region of the East China Sea experienced considerable European contact during the 16th century. The Portuguese arrived in China in 1508, reached the Moluccas (Indonesia) in 1511, and then landed in Japan in 1543. Because of the superiority of their ships and weapons, the Portuguese became the "primary carriers of goods in the East Asian trade" (Shirokauer, 1978: 308). They established trading stations everywhere, and in 1557 were allowed to open such a station in Macao on the Chinese mainland. The Portuguese combined piracy with trading and must have been familiar with Okinawa and the Ryukyu Islands. Their weapons and fighting techniques would have been known in every country bordering the East and South China Seas.

The Spanish moved into the Philippines in 1565, and had conquered most of the Philippine lowlands by the end of that century. The original arnis in the Philippines was named *espada y daga* by the Spaniards and is still known under this name today (Draeger & Smith, 1980: 188), and Mark Wiley (1994: 23) states that the Spanish two handed system of rapier and dagger had considerable influence on the development of *esgrima* (a Spanish word meaning "fencing"). So we know that these European techniques were well known in the Philippines.

For a while there was a great deal of Japanese interest in European things, including weapons and fencing technique. In 1615, Hasekura Tsunenaga (1571–1622) led a party of 68 Japanese to Europe to study the customs of those countries for the Shogun of Japan (Sasamori & Warner, 1964: 48). Hasekura was a noted swordsman, and his group stayed in Europe for five years. Rapier and dagger techniques were popular in Europe well into the 17th century. When Hasekura returned to Japan, he was most assuredly familiar with the left-hand dagger and its use. It is evident that sword and dagger fighting would have been well known in East Asia, especially in Japan, before the Europeans were virtually driven out around 1638.

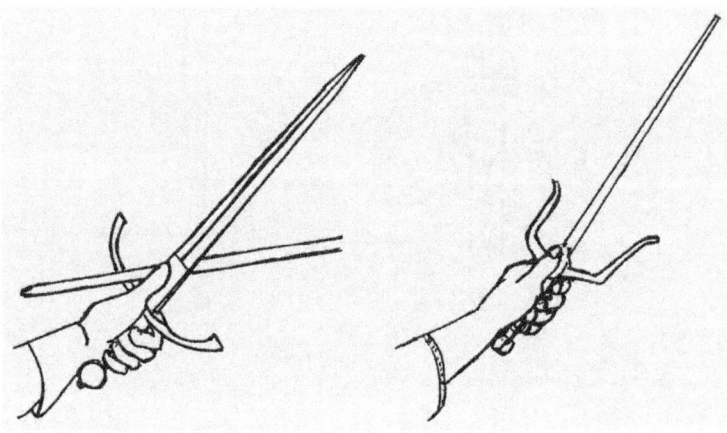

Left-hand dagger parrying a thrust
(after Wagner, 1979).
Sai in "furi" position.

The similarity of the left hand dagger, especially one possessing a simple guard and a poniard blade, to East Asian trident spear heads may have suggested dismounting those spearheads for use in the hand. Certainly, we cannot dismiss, out of hand so to speak, the possible origin of the sai as a left-hand weapon to complement a sword in the other hand. The coastal inhabitants of the China seas had the opportunity to closely observe European fencing techniques and the use of the left hand dagger. If, as has been asserted by Matayoshi and Sakagami, the sai point was originally sharp, saijutsu may have initially contained a number of lethal thrusting techniques which are no longer taught.

Okinawa

Okinawa is the largest island in the Ryukyu Archipelago and has a very favorable position on the maritime trade routes between Korea/Japan and South China. Okinawa is long and thin, and so everywhere is close to the sea. Being mostly coastline, with good natural harbors, ships stop at the island for food, water, trade, and shelter. These East Asian waters are also notorious for piracy and have been for centuries. And when piracy was slack, the Ryukyu Islands would offer an opportunity for a little coastal pillaging. The pillaging of coastal villages, if repeated, can generate an awful lot of local enthusiasm among the villagers for martial arts training, i.e. the early Okinawan fighting arts (te).

Okinawa is subtropical in both vegetation and climate. The island has no metal ores and is largely limestone. The soils are fertile, and the island was forested. If you want to use iron for tools or weapons, the iron must be imported, and of course it's not cheap. Unless you want to spend a lot of money, you use the resources which are locally available. Wood was very popular.

During the Chinese Ming dynasty, about 1350 CE or so, Okinawa was divided into three independent antagonistic kingdoms. When one of those kings realized the value of Chinese protection for his kingdom, he became a vassal of China. The advantages of this protection became immediately obvious to the other two kings, and soon the entire island was under nominal Chinese suzerainty. As commerce followed politics, trade developed between Okinawa and China and continued, more or less continuously, for the next 500 years.

In 1470, the second Sho Dynasty was established in Okinawa and reigned until 1879. During the 16th century, the island became wealthy because of its strategic trade position in the East China Sea. The introduction of the sai to Okinawa, regardless of its point of origin may be assumed to have occurred during the Sho dynasty, and it has been commonly maintained that in ca. 1480, the third king in that dynasty banned all personal weapons. If so, this might have some bearing on the history of the sai, but there is evidence that no such ban ever existed (Kerr & Sakihara, 2000: 543–544).

In 1609, the Satsuma [Shimazu] clan from southern Japan invaded Okinawa and the Okinawan king became a puppet under that clan's political control. On occasion an Okinawan king would be sent to exile in Japan and replaced by a more pliable member of his family. But, until 1879 there was always someone on the Okinawan throne requiring personal security.

In 1699, the Satsuma supposedly banned all weapons and their importation, and enforced the ban. In fact, there was a series of actions, a ban on weapons export to Ryukyu in 1639, abolishment of government sword manufacture at Shuri in 1669, and a second ban on shipment of weapons to Ryukyu in 1699, but it would seem that there was never an actual ban on weapons on Okinawa itself (Kerr & Sakihara, 2000: 544).[11] Even during the Satsuma era, the Chinese maintained their commercial ties and a sort of political "shadow" presence on the island. However, the arrival of the Satsuma barred the Okinawan nobility from many of their former occupations and created an increasing number of leisured, moneyed, and bored aristocrats who could go to China and study the Chinese language, classics, and martial arts. A number of young men did go, and some of them became very proficient indeed.

Some Okinawan authorities maintain that the sai was derived from an agricultural implement for cutting a furrow or poking holes in the ground for seeds. In fact, a sort of dibble. If these authorities are correct, we could translate "sai" as dibble, and saijutsu as "dibble art." Now "dibble" is a fine English word going back to at least the 15th century, but it does lack a certain dignity.

This odd fiction of Okinawan peasant origin is much sillier than Yang's hairpin story. As a long pointed stick would do the same job without constant bending and would be much cheaper, this dibble derivation is unlikely. At least its use as a hairpin accounts for the tines, which are such an important part of the weapon and which have no conceivable use on the farm implement. If the sai were merely a dibble, then those odd prongs would vanish to save metal and money.

The Okinawan peasant did not practice martial arts. He would have neither the time, money, nor the permission to train. But, when you live someplace that is mostly coastline, farming is generally a way to have something to eat with your fish. So there were a lot of fishermen, and out at sea they were more vulnerable to the odd passing pirate. Fishermen would have a little more money and leisure time than peasants, a lot more incentive to learn self-defense, and seamen in general tend to be more aggressive and more open to new ideas than peasants. It would be strange indeed if this sea-going Okinawan "lower" class was unable to fight. Equivalent socially to the peasant class, Okinawan sailors and fishermen may be the basis for the stories of the unarmed and armed fighting arts (*te* and *kobu*) originating as peasant arts. Still, it is not likely that Okinawan fishermen developed the sai. The barbed trident is a fisherman's tool, an unbarbed trident would be much less useful.

The sai was not normally an urban civilian weapon. A difficult weapon to use, it takes considerable training to attain skill at even a basic level. The weapon is not cheap, and it does not have any other use except as a weapon. Its weight and awkwardness when carried would be its most important drawback to itinerant priests, Zen or otherwise. Although a sai can easily be carried stuck through a sash, three of them carried that way, almost six pounds of ironmongery, would be a considerable nuisance while walking any distance. For the average thief or bandit, there are many weapons which are less obvious, more lethal, and easier to carry. Because it is not a bladed weapon and the point is blunt, the sai is not a military weapon; besides, the military profession on Okinawa was restricted to the Japanese. Nor is it a weapon, which would be carried by those Japanese civilian classes with the right to bear arms. They carried real swords.

The sai had to be an Okinawan police and security weapon, and the official use of such arms must have had at least the tacit approval of the Satsuma. What could be a more natural common ground for the Okinawan aristocracy and the heads of the Satsuma than an interest in preserving domestic peace, welfare, and the status quo? Okinawan ingenuity in arming their police and security personnel while avoiding the prohibited blades was considerable. Witness the immense popularity, which the modern *tonfa* (PR-24 baton) has acquired among police agencies in the last quarter of the 20th century. The staff (*bo*) was also a formidable police weapon in Okinawa and Japan. It too was never a farm implement.

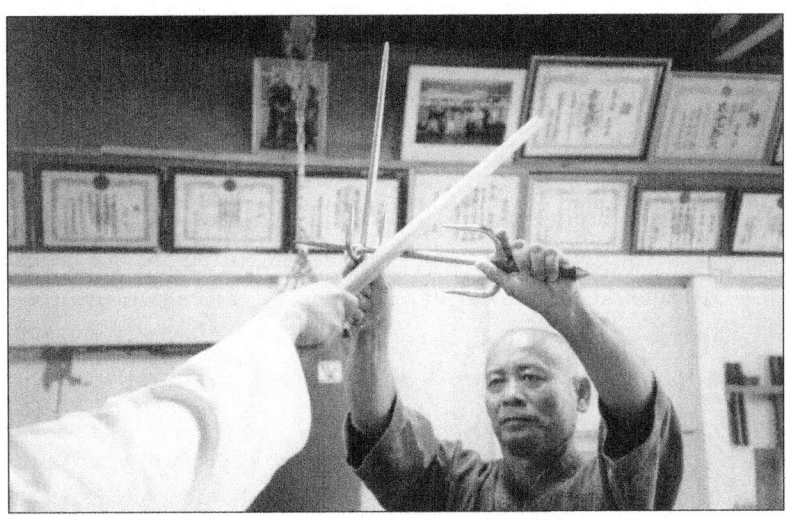

A leading representative of the Okinawan martial traditions, Kinjo Takashi presents a version of an upper-block. Notice how he uses the right sai's tine to support the left sai's shaft. Photo courtesy of Mary Bolz.

Tentative Conclusions

This history of the sai suggests that both Okinawan unarmed (*te*, *tode*, *uchinadi*) and armed (*kobudo*) fighting arts developed from weapons and techniques originally brought from China by mid-level Okinawan aristocracy and adapted in Okinawa to serve as police and security measures for self-defense, protection of VIP's, and maintenance of public order. This is a very significant observation of considerable general importance to the study of the Okinawan martial arts. It explains much.

I suspect that the epithet "peasant" applied to the Okinawa martial arts originated in a Japanese bias in favor of their own powerful martial traditions and a certain degree of prejudice against the Ryukyu islanders. The Okinawans certainly knew better. This samurai prejudice may well have been encouraged by demonstrations rigged as a matter of policy by the Okinawans to show a marked inferiority on the part of Okinawan weapons and techniques. This interpretation is supported by the secrecy with which instruction was carried out during most of the 19th century. If these techniques and weapons weren't actually forbidden to the general public, certainly every effort was made to restrict the number of people who were proficient. This reticence is well explained by official efforts to keep the Japanese from understanding the effectiveness of Okinawan unarmed and armed fighting arts. Certainly no responsible ruler or police official wanted his officers disarmed because the occupying power felt their weapons were a potential threat to its position.

If all or even most of the traditional Okinawan weapons were originally for police use only, then these weapons were very rarely used against each other. When looking at a police weapon, its effectiveness must be evaluated against weapons which the police could expect to encounter. Doing so eliminates applications against most other weapons or against a warrior's sword. Instead, as noted above, they would have been used against the edged and impact weapons favored by the pirates of the China seas and against unarmed and untrained men. This historical insight is vitally important to our understanding of basic techniques and kata sequences in all the Okinawan martial arts, especially for those Okinawan katas practiced before 1870. All modern interpretations of applications should be re-examined in these terms.

Because of the coincidence in dates with the historical appearance of the sai in Okinawa, two traditions are suspected of having contributed to the original development of the sai and its techniques: first, the trident spear spreading from India through Indonesia and throughout East Asia; and second, left hand dagger techniques spreading from Iberian Europe through the Philippines, China, or Japan, suggesting that the trident spearhead be dismounted and held in the hand for defensive use.

The available evidence strongly suggests that the sai was originally a trident spearhead imported to Okinawa from China. It was then modified (possibly immediately) in Okinawa for elite police, bodyguards, or other peacekeeping personnel. The fully developed sai would be an excellent weapon for keeping order among semi-piratical ships' crews enjoying the delights of the Okinawan waterfronts. The sai would also help provide adequate defense for royal (or other important) persons against assault. As the idea was to apprehend malefactors for the mills of justice or potential assassins for interrogation, the sai would be a better choice than a bladed weapon. The iron sai would also be an intimidating weapon for use during periods of civil disorder.

I suggest dividing the history of the sai in Okinawa into three periods:

1) Importation and Development (1675–1699)
2) Satsuma Weapons Ban (1699)
   Use as a Police/Security Weapon (1699–1870)
3) Meiji Restoration (1868)
   Civilian Weapon (1870–present)

Nishiuchi Mikio, president of the International Okinawan Kobudo Association, U.S.A., demonstrates sai techniques against swordsman Dale Sussdorf. Such techniques may have evolved from earlier sai techniques. Photo by Taira Yoshimura & courtesy of Mary Bolz.

The dates seem artificially precise, but the importance of the two pivotal years, 1699 and 1868, is no exaggeration. Supposedly the import of all weapons (one supposes including trident spearheads) into Okinawa was forbidden after 1699, and in 1868, the loss of samurai privileges, the adoption of 19th century police methods, and the liberalization of society brought the fighting arts wider popularity.

The first of these three periods is vague and the date 1675 is only a guess, but we have two important men who lived during this period, Hamahiga and Shitahaku Oyakata.[12] It is quite possible that the sai was known and in use on Okinawa well before 1675, but we have no evidence to support this early presence. This may be due simply to an understandable loss of oral tradition with time, or there may have been no sais in use to leave evidence. Proving the latter would be very difficult and to compound the problem, the weapon may have been known but not in use by the Okinawans throughout the 16th and early 17th centuries.

This historical explanation is offered merely as a plausible hypothesis. There is still much work to be done on the history of this fascinating weapon. Because today the sai is also widely used outside of Okinawa, we should also investigate its origins from the perspective of earlier conditions existing in these other countries as well. Original trident spears and nuntes should be aged, described carefully, and photographed. Okinawan archives need to be searched for biographical and administrative details concerning the royal bodyguards and the Okinawan police. A careful survey should be made throughout Southeast Asia regarding the presence of the sai and its use in other martial arts traditions. We must also ask if it is possible that the sai spread from Okinawa more recently to be adopted in its current form elsewhere in east Asia. Hopefully many uncertainties will be eliminated by future research of this kind.

Acknowledgments

My special thanks to Mario McKenna, who supplied me with the material and references to the Japanese language texts cited in this article. I would also like to thank Joe Swift for permission to use his translation of the passage from Nakamoto's book. Richard Florence also made several very useful contributions. Without their generous help, this article would have been much the poorer.

Notes

1. RRB = Rapid Rotational Baton manufactured by RRB Systems International in Jacksonville, FL.
2. *Ufuchiku* is an old Okinawan police rank, often regarded as equivalent to the British ranks of "senior inspector" or "chief inspector." This equivalency is not exact, so it would be better merely to consider a man with such a rank as a very senior police official. *Chikusaji* is another old Okinawan police rank, but junior to the ufuchiku.
3. Nakamoto Masahiro (1983). *Okinawa dento kobudo: Sono Rekishi to Tamashii*. Naha: Okiinsha. p. 85. Translation provided by Mr. Charles Joseph Swift.
4. The *Peichin* were members of a class of the Okinawan aristocracy apparently responsible for domestic security and public order.
5. Kim (1974: 9) says that Yara Chatan was a young man in the year 1700. However, it seems that there were two men named Yara who lived about 100 years apart and were both of the Peichin class. We are concerned here with Yara "Chatan," who was born in Chatan village in 1741. It is believed that Yara Chatan developed the kobudo katas which bear his name, but this cannot be confirmed. Chatan Yara is frequently confused (Bishop, 1989: 79; Nagamine, 2000: 84) with "Yomitan" Yara of Yomitan village who is said to have instructed Kyan Chotoku (Mario McKenna, personal communication).
6. This readiness to adapt kata and techniques is supportive evidence for the modification of Chinese martial arts for specific Okinawan purposes, i.e. law enforcement and security.
7. Okinawan sai masters are all karate masters as well.
8. Further investigation is necessary to examine the similarities between thrusts with the sai and thrusts with the European left hand dagger.
9. We need to know if these statues show the trident spear or the shorter, hand-held sai.
10. Possibly the murals and statues at Borobudur and the Prambanan Temple complex in Central Java (Draeger, 1972: 23). Unfortunately none of the statues he depicts in his book show the sai.
11. From Sakihara's statements, it would appear that these weapons regulations specifically banned export of weapons from Japan to Ryukyu. It seems likely that if that were the entire intent of these regulations, they would have affected neither the importation of weapons from China nor the ownership of weapons on Okinawa itself. These points need to be cleared up.
12. Kim (1974: 17) states that Shitahaku Oyakata is an area of Okinawa, not a person. This statement illustrates the confusion which exists today among supposedly authoritative historical sources in English. See Taira Shinken's writings translated by Patrick McCarthy (1969).

Bibliography

Bishop, M. (1989). *Okinawan karate: Teachers, styles, and secret techniques.* London: A & C Black.

Bishop, M. (1996). *Zen kobudo: Mysteries of Okinawan weaponry and te.* Rutland, VT: Tuttle Publishing.

Corcoran, J. & Farkas, E. (1993). *The original martial arts encyclopedia.* Los Angeles, CA: Pro-Action Publishing.

Crosswell, R. (1993). Okinawan kobudo: "The other wheel". *Fighting Arts International,* 81: 50–51.

Demura, F. (1974). *Sai: karate weapon of self-defense.* Santa Clarita, CA: Ohara.

Draeger, D. (1972). *The weapons and fighting arts of Indonesia.* Rutland, VT: Tuttle Publishing.

Draeger, D. & Smith, R. (1980). *Comprehensive Asian fighting arts.* Toyko: Kodansha International.

Hergsell, G. (1998). *Tallhoffer's fechtbuch.* Herne, Germany: VS-Books.

Kerr, G. & Sakihara, M. (2000). *Okinawa: The history of an island people.* Rutland, VT: Tuttle.

Kim, R. (1974). *The weaponless warriors.* Santa Clarita, CA: Ohara.

Kim, R. (1983). *Kobudo 1: Okinawan weapons of Matsu Higa.* Hamilton, Ontario: Masters Publications.

Kim, R. (1985). *Kobudo 2: Okinawan weapons of Hama Higa.* Hamilton, Ontario: Masters Publications.

Matayoshi, S. (1995a). *Okinawan kobudo: Part 1* (video). Thousand Oaks, CA: Tsunami.

Matayoshi, S. (1995b). *Okinawan kobudo: Part 2* (video). Thousand Oaks, CA: Tsunami.

McCarthy, P. (Trans.) (1999). *Ancient Okinawan martial arts. Koryu uchinadi, vol. 1.* Rutland, VT: Tuttle Publishing.

McCarthy, P. (Trans.) (1999). *Ancient Okinawan martial arts. Koryu uchinadi, vol. 2.* Rutland, VT: Tuttle Publishing.

Murakami, K. (2000). *Saijutsu: Traditional Okinawan weapon art.* Rutland, VT: Tuttle Publishing.

Nagamine, S. (McCarthy, P., Trans.) (2000). *Tales of Okinawa's great masters.* Rutland, VT: Tuttle Publishing.

Oshiro T. (1998). *Uchinadi II.* (video). Thousand Oaks, CA: Tsunami.

Pant, G. (1978, 1980, 1983). *Indian arms and armour.* 3 Volumes. New Delhi, India: Army Educational Stores.

Parulski, G. (1984). *The art of karate weapons.* Chicago: Contemporary Publications.

Sakagami, R. (n.d.). *Sai of Tsukenshitahaku*. Tokyo: Ogawa Trading Company.

Sakagami, R. (1974). *Nunchaku and sai: Ancient Okinawan martial arts*. Tokyo: Japan Publications.

Sasamori, J. & Warner, G. (1964). *This is kendo*. Rutland, VT: Tuttle.

Sells, J. (1998). Karate kobudo: A personal view. *Furyu: The Budo Journal*. (9): 43.

Shirokauer, C. (1978). *A brief history of Chinese and Japanese civilizations*. New York: Harcourt Brace and Jovanovitch.

Stone, G. (1961, 1934). *A glossary of the construction, decoration, and use of arms and armour*. New York: Jack Brussel Publisher.

Wagner, E. (1979). *Weapons & warfare; 1618–1648*. London: Octopus Books.

Wiley, M. (1994). *Filipino martial arts*. Rutland, VT: Tuttle Publishing.

Yang, J. (1999). *Ancient Chinese weapons*. Boston, MA: YMAA Publication Center.

The Walking Stick: The Gentleman's Weapon

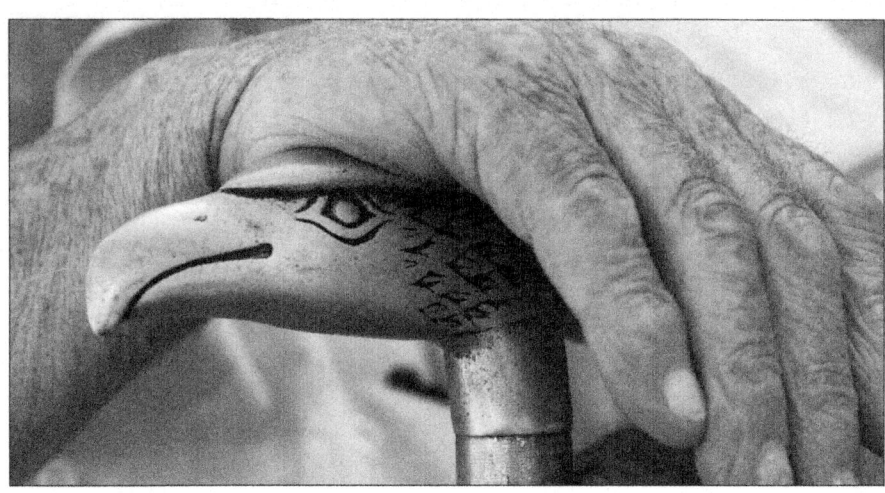

Introduction

There are several factors that call for treating the walking stick as a separate weapon in the context of fighting arts. The average walking stick is different in size, balance, and reach when compared to all other stick weapons, and it has never been standardized. It can't be. It possesses a distinct handle that varies in size and shape according to the taste and physique of its owner, and its length is determined by the height at which it can be used for comfortable support when held by that handle. The stick must fit its owner. This point is very important. It means that there is an almost infinite variety of walking sticks differing in materials, length, strength, weight, balance, and handle type. It is a more individual weapon than most, and this affects training and practice.

In civilian self-defense, the basic strategic problem is to evade an unprovoked and unexpected attack, disengage from the assailant, and escape the situation. The problem's precise tactical solution depends on your abilities and on attack specifics. The classical Asian fighting arts were devised solely to enable you to survive such an attack by giving you skills to load the odds in your favor. The possession of a walking stick increases this "edge."

Walking stick training offers major advantages over most other forms of self-defense:

- A walking stick or cane provides a reasonable defense against an attack by an untrained dog, and even some larger breeds can be kept at a distance.

- The basic techniques are simple, so it is possible to develop an effective defense faster than with unarmed combatives.
- These skills require less maintenance than those of combatives. Hours of weekly training are not necessary to retain defensive capability.
- The techniques are powerful. The stick multiplies the force of the blows, providing much of the focus and impact. This too cuts back on the amount of training required.
- The length of the stick gives an important extension in reach.
- With proper training, the stick allows effective defense without the necessity for lethal force. Nevertheless, the walking stick increases impact so that a blow that would merely be painful if struck with the hand may cause dangerous or lethal injury if struck with a stick. All thrusts are potentially lethal.
- A walking stick is not legally considered a weapon and it may be openly and habitually carried or "worn," as the older expression has it, especially by the weak, aged, or infirm as a recognized and significant aide to locomotion.
- You can carry it with you everywhere as an aide to walking, which allows you to become more intimately familiar with it than with most other weapons.

Although in case of need a walking stick or cane[1] can be a superb defensive weapon for the average civilian, that is not its primary function. Basically, it is an extremely versatile aide for walkers, particularly on hills and stairs. It improves balance. It gives additional purchase on wet, icy, or slippery terrain. Going up hill, it provides support and takes pressure from the back and hips, reducing stress on those parts of the body. It is very helpful traversing a hillside, and it protects the knees when going down hill. It has a host of other practical uses as well. The walking stick is a means for effective defense that may be kept constantly to hand. This fact alone should make it the weapon of choice for any civilian who feels the need of protection against attack. Why is this not the case?

One major reason for the scarcity of walking sticks is fashion. Today, people generally don't walk much, so the stick is no longer fashionable. Although some people have rediscovered its utility, few today stroll on street or trail for their individual pleasure using a stick for solid support and companionship. Another reason is urban crowding. It can be difficult to manipulate or carry a stick in a crowded mall or elevator without unintentionally poking someone. In life, just as in any fighting art, courtesy and regard for others is extremely important.

Yet another major reason for its neglect is that the walking stick's defensive capabilities are generally misunderstood, and it can be very difficult to find effective, simple training. Today, there are few instructors of defensive technique for the walking stick, and most of those aren't very good. Although some training from other forms of defense may usefully transfer to the walking stick, most do not. Use of a walking stick is neither unarmed combat nor fencing, and few martial artists or fencers are familiar with proper walking stick techniques.

Although the European fencer has a considerable advantage over other martial artists when learning the stick, and some techniques may even be identical, especially for the saber fencer, the stick is a more versatile and complex weapon than a sword. It does not possess a hand guard and the grip, distancing, timing, stance, and targets are different. Unlike the fencer, you don't fight in a straight line, and you can forget the lunge altogether.

Cane or walking stick instruction is often embedded in an empty-hand fighting art, and Asian martial arts instructors often regard cane lessons as an advanced aspect of their art, subordinate to empty-hand techniques. When this is the case, much of the cane's effectiveness and simplicity is lost, and lessons are rarely given. In addition, I must stress that cane fighting is not merely karate or taekwondo with a stick in your hand. For the most effective and efficient instruction, the cane or walking stick must be taught separately, not as a part of another fighting art.

The karate practitioner can sometimes blend karate and stick fighting to advantage, but he must use his karate to increase his stick's effectiveness, not the other way around. Any weapon makes its possessor much more dangerous in a fight, so if a karate practitioner has a stick, it becomes his basic weapon and its characteristics control the way he fights. As in fencing, distancing, timing, stance, and targets are different.

This is not meant to imply that there is no valid instruction for the walking stick available in the Asian fighting arts. There is and it can be very good indeed, but it is rare. And there can be a lot of rubbish to clear away before you get to it. Special uniforms, ranks, insignia, organization, group training, or competitions are all irrelevant. They get in the way of realistic training. They distract. They hinder. Avoid them. As the walking stick is used for effective self-defense with a minimum of training, to require more than necessary is self-defeating.

Fighting Styles

The word "cane" appears to derive from the Latin word "*canis*" meaning "for a dog,"[2] which indicates the first defensive use for European walking sticks (Monek, 1995: 21–22). This derivation suggests that the Romans, an urban people, were either the first to use it defensively, which is unlikely, or that they used it a lot, and that it was primarily a defense against loose, vicious dogs. This is more likely. The longer staff was more of a rural implement.

The "single stick" was used in prizefights, but is not a true cane weapon. Photograph courtesy of R. Dohrenwend.

Historically, the walking stick has been highly regarded as a defensive weapon in Europe. One author has even suggested that Irish blackthorn stick fighting be given the status of a national martial art (Hurley, 2001). In any case, it is generally believed that the walking stick is primarily a European weapon and that the most effective techniques for its use were developed in France. This belief is probably correct. Because of its effectiveness, at certain periods in most European countries, members of the general populace were forbidden to carry a walking stick. During the French Revolution, people were again allowed to carry walking sticks, but Napoleon revoked this permission in 1804. This general prohibition was one of the laws that led to the revolutionary convulsions across Europe during 1848 (Klever, 1984: 30). After that year, carrying a walking stick became generally legal and extremely common.

During the second half of the 19th century, the walking stick in Europe and North America was a gentleman's constant companion. Throughout that ill-policed era, it was regarded as essential protection against footpads, ruffians, and hooligans; and there were attempts, some of them quite good, to develop a formal fighting art based on the walking stick. Various "schools" emerged during this era in France, Spain, Italy, Britain, Germany and elsewhere. The walking stick's popularity in Europe as a gentleman's defense during the Victorian era coincided with the greatest period of European expansion and influence in south and east Asia. The officers and entrepreneurs of the various imperial nations certainly brought their canes and stick-fighting techniques east with them. European influence must be acknowledged when evaluating Asian cane techniques today.

During this era, the famous English "single stick" was at first a weapon to replace the more deadly sword in prizefights, and then became a training weapon for the cavalry saber. The kind of rustic entertainment, so well described in Hughes' *Tom Brown's School Days*, is an obvious relic of the single stick's earlier use in prizefights. Indeed, that form of stick play was still called "backswording." However, the single stick normally possesses a hand guard and hilt, and cannot be considered a true cane weapon.

E. W. Barton-Wright (1860–1951), creator of the eclectic art of Bartitsu, utilized the walking stick in his self-defense practice.

European walking stick technique reached its greatest sophistication in France's *la canne*, which was normally taught as part of savate. At the beginning of the 20th century, its most noted instructor, Pierre Vigny, taught his walking stick techniques as a part of the "Bartitsu" style of fighting developed by the somewhat eccentric Englishman, E. W. Barton-Wright. The horrific slaughter inflicted on France during the Great War (1914–1918) almost extinguished savate and virtually wiped out instructors and participants in *la canne*. After the war, the cane's popularity as a walking aid rapidly waned as the bicycle and then the auto became increasingly common. *La canne* was on the point of vanishing completely as a fighting art, when it underwent a revival, developing a new identity as a combat sport.

Photographs illustrating the use of the walking stick for self-defense as developed by Barton-Wright.

Five years after the end of the Great War, H.G. Lang, a British officer in the Indian Police, introduced the walking stick to his force and gave organized instruction in its use. His methods were based on Pierre Vigny's and were designed as a serious combative. He wrote a fine little book on the subject, *The Walking Method of Self-Defense* (1923), and judging from the enthusiastic praise in the preface, it was very well received. His system was even taught to Indian Boy Scouts.

While the European styles and schools have generally decayed and largely vanished since the Great War, Asian instruction has been preserved, improved, and, although still uncommon, can be found today. When we think of Asian techniques for a walking stick or stick, we immediately think of the Philippine *arnis* or *esgrima/eskrima*. Its effectiveness is uncontested and it offers a superb basis for cane/walking stick instruction. Outside of the Philippines, Asian martial arts training with the cane is limited and Asian instructors in other traditions are not as familiar with this weapon. Mostly, they train far less with the cane than they do with their unarmed techniques.

Hapkido is a relatively modern and eclectic Korean fighting art. Because the art is new, it was able to adopt the crook-handled cane and develop innovative techniques (*tan jang sul*) for its use right from the very beginning. Although the Hapkido's *tan jang sul* offers very effective instruction in the crook-handled cane, the style unfortunately treats the cane as an advanced weapon and many of the techniques taught will only work for a highly trained person. As the crook-handled cane is definitely a supplement to this style, with the Koreans understandably and naturally relying more on Hapkido's core techniques, they have not yet fully developed the cane's potential.

In Japan, the walking stick is a relatively neglected weapon compared to the sophisticated instruction available for the six-foot (*bo*) and four-foot staffs (*jo*). Nevertheless, the Japanese have developed techniques for the three-foot stick (*hanbo*, "half staff") taught in aikido and the more classic Kukishin-Ryu jujutsu. Those techniques deserve serious study. Publicly taught classic technique emphasizes a two-handed grip, short-end pressure-point applications, and immobilizations. There are also some useful techniques for releasing a captured stick.

Aikido's *hanbo* is used more as a lever than an impact weapon, with considerable emphasis on locks and immobilizations. Techniques seem to involve grasping the stick toward the middle or in both hands, sacrificing reach and impact. Although the techniques are elegant and effective, they rely on the stick as a supplement to unarmed technique, requiring more training than necessary for effective civilian defense. This would suggest that the Japanese techniques are designed for police rather than civilian use (Hatsumi & Chambers, 1971).

Uchida Ryugoro (1837–1921) offers a superb example of the European origins and influence on the Asian development of walking-stick techniques. Between 1854 and 1859, he developed one-handed techniques for the European walking stick (a straight, tapered stick, about 90 cm long). His son, Uchida Ryohei, later codified these techniques as Uchida-Ryu tanjojutsu, and assembled 12 forms (*katas*) of one to three moves each. The only Japanese weapons art of European origin, even sometimes called *suteki* (English stick) *jutsu*, it is now taught as supplemental instruction in Shindo Muso-Ryu jojutsu.

The walking stick (Mandarin: *guai gun*) is also used in Chinese taijiquan.[4] There is at least one elegant and useful taiji solo form for this weapon which is derived from a two-person drill (Gilman, 2003). The straight stick is used, and the techniques and their applications are strong and deceptively simple. Where there is one such exercise, there are more, and if that form is indicative of general Chinese understanding of the walking stick as a weapon, the Chinese are very knowledgeable indeed.

TECHNICAL SECTION
Hapkido Techniques
Illustrations & text courtesy of Marc Tedeschi
www.tedeschi-media.com

Side Step + Combination Strikes

Adopt a relaxed stance and side-handle grip (A). As attacker punches, step laterally with your left foot and execute a lateral strike to their wrist (B–C), or an outside block with the shaft. Without pausing, swing the cane over your head, turn the handle against the back of your wrist (D), and execute an outside circular strike to the temple (E). Allow the strike's motion to position the cane for the next strike (F). Follow with an Inside circular strike to the inner knee (G).

Important Points

This combination of strikes is characterized by a continuous series of circular whipping motions that are very fast. Properly done, you should hear whistling as the cane cuts through the air. You can easily lengthen this combination by adding additional circular strikes. Alternating between high and low targets makes it more difficult for your opponent to block or avoid your blows, and hinders their ability to grab your cane.

Strike + Passing Arm Bar

Attacker steps forward with a right punch. Step to their inside with your right foot (A–B). Parry and grab their wrist with your left hand, as you deliver an inside strike to the ribs (C). Step inward with your left foot, as you pass your arm and the cane under attacker's elbow, leaving the end of the shaft firmly planted against attacker's abdomen. Lock their elbow by pressing upward and backward with the shaft and your inner elbow, as you push their wrist in the opposite direction (D). Step under their arm with your right foot and pivot 180°, twisting their arm as you go (E). Lift their wrist as you press the shaft downward into the elbow, locking the joint as you lever the end of the cane into their chest (F).

Important Points

Try to lock attacker's elbow by step D, since this makes it more difficult for them to counter as you pass under their arm. After applying the arm bar (F), you can force attacker to their knees or belly if needed. Do this by pulling them off-balance toward their front or right front-corner as you apply the arm bar.

Taijiquan Techniques

Illustrations & text courtesy of Michael Gilman • www.gilmanstudios.com

Partner Sequence

A) *On Guard Position:* Michael Gilman (R) and Stephanie Morrell in this typical preparation stance.

B) *Look for the Snake:* Morrell (L) brings her cane up, protecting her head while she steps in for the attack.

C) *Look for the Snake* continues: Morrell strikes toward Gilman's knee.

D) *Ride the Tiger:* Gilman lifts his right leg out of the way and blocks the strike to his right in preparation for his follow up attack.

E) *Eagle Spreads It's Wing:* Gilman follows immediately with a strike to Morrell's temple.
F) *Rising Stick:* Morrell retreats out of range and neutralizes Gilman's strike. Partners are again in *On Guard*.
G) *Whirlwind:* Morrell presses down slightly on Gilman's cane in preparation for a strike to Gilman's temple.
H) *Whirlwind* continues with Morrell striking toward Gilman's temple.
I) *Dragon Attacks:* Gilman ducks down to avoid the strike and protects his head.
J) *Dragon Attacks* continues with Gilman striking toward Morrell's knee.

K) *Ride the Wind:* Morrell steps backwards, getting her knee out of the way, and knocks Gilman's cane to her right.

L) Finishing *Dragon Attacks*, Gilman follows up by stepping in and attacking Morrell's temple. Gilman would then step back into the starting *On Guard* position.

Photography by Susan Linebach.

Stick Selection

Any stick will do in an emergency, but just as with any other weapon you must be familiar with materials and characteristics to properly select one for defensive use. A cane may be made from a single piece of wood, in which case it is called a "self" cane or stick. If the handle is made of another material, the cane is of "composite" construction. If the structure of the shaft is the same as when it was grown, having essentially the same diameter, with growth rings forming concentric circles around the pith, it is called a "stem" cane and good examples are the Irish blackthorn and the Basque *makhila*. Most walking sticks, however, are "turned" to the proper shape on a lathe.

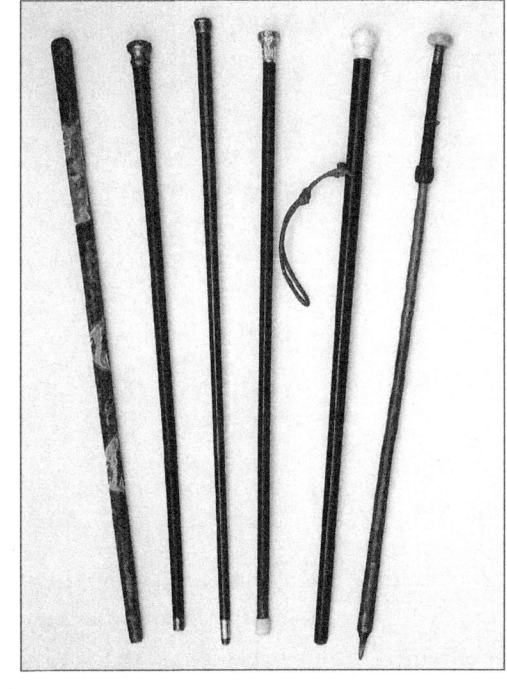

Straight antique walking sticks suitable for self-defense, dating from the mid-19th to the early 20th century. The stick on the far right is a Basque makhila.

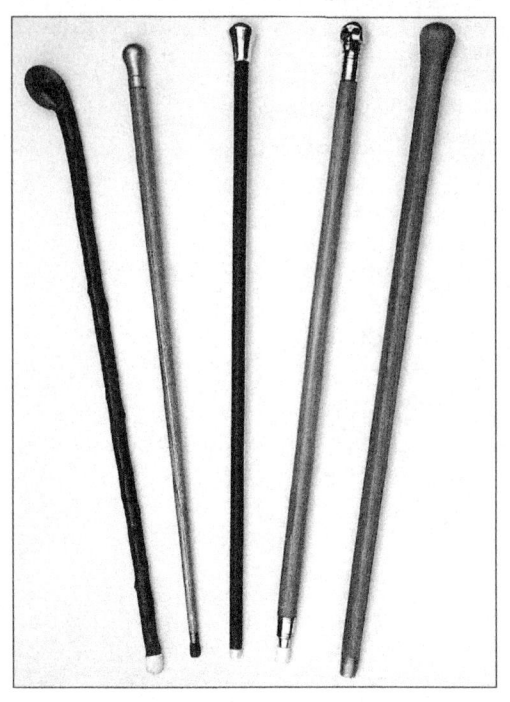

Straight modern walking sticks suitable for self-defense. The stick on the far left is an Irish blackthorn. The stick next to it is the superb Walking Stick™ model.

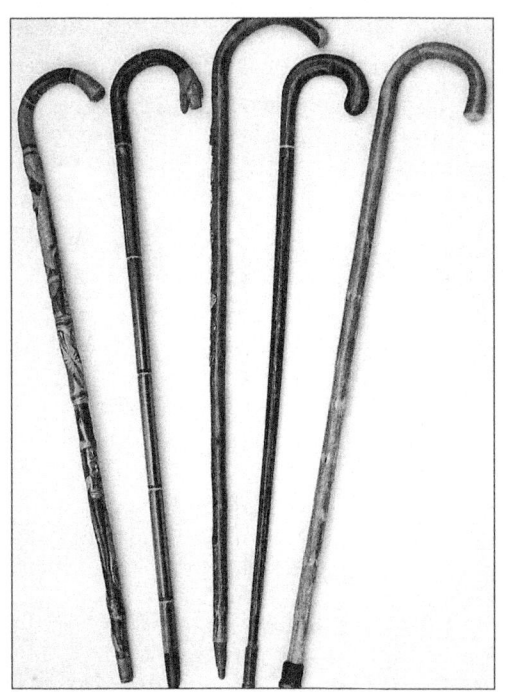

Crook-handled walking sticks suitable for self-defense. The crook handle on the old German Spazierstock in the middle has slightly straightened with years. *Photographs courtesy of R. Dohrenwend.*

Handles and Balance

There is a large variety of handle materials, weights, and shapes. The most satisfactory types for defense are the knob and crook handles.[3] Both provide a secure grip, and the crook may also offer some protection to the hand holding the cane. Some very fast, elegant, and attractive techniques are possible with a crook handle. Nevertheless, the hooking techniques permitted by the crook handle are of limited practicality. They require a high level of skill, practice, and fitness to work reliably, and if extended toward an opponent, the crook makes it easier for him to grab your stick and disarm you.

The stick should be light and balanced so that the point end can be wielded with speed and precision. The walking stick should feel "alive" in the hand. A straight stick balanced toward the center has to be held close to that balance point for speed, thus you lose reach. A knob or pommel of heavier material moves the balance back toward the handle, as does a taper from pommel to point. This superior balance, which is the main purpose of a heavy pommel, gives the cane greater impact and reach, and faster recovery. It is also harder for an opponent to take your cane away.

Materials

A very wide variety of woods[4] have been used for making satisfactory walking sticks. Five of the very best are blackthorn (*Prunus spinosa*) and medlar (*Mespilus germanica*) for "stem" walking sticks; and shagbark hickory (*Carya ovata*), white ash (*Fraxinus americana*), and black locust (*Robinia pseudoacacia*) for "turned" walking sticks. All of these woods are very strong and elastic, but the preferred wood for an impact tool or weapon is rapid growth (not more than 16 rings to the inch) sap wood hickory. It should be straight grained, smooth, and free from knots or other defects. A hickory shaft with sharply contrasting color figure, containing heartwood, is prettier but more likely to split.

Grain straightness is very important for a turned stick. The grain lines should run straight from the pommel to the tip. The shaft's taper will cause the outside lines to fade out creating a "feathering" effect on two opposite sides of the shaft. Cane shafts with diagonal grain will break more easily than shafts with straight grain.

Rattan ("Malacca"), which comes from the palm genus *Calamus* (not a bamboo), is another fine material for the shafts of walking sticks and canes, and during the 15th century was the most highly valued of all. However, as rattan is an imprecise term including nine genera of climbing palms found throughout Southeast Asia and Indonesia, it is likely that most have been used for "Malacca" walking sticks at one time or another. It is usually not possible to tell even the genus of palm from which a stick is made, but the most desirable rattan for walking sticks has widely separated joints or nodes and is called *rotan semambu*.

Today, of course, there are also many excellent artificial materials available: resin impregnated woods, plastics, carbon fibers, fiberglass, and composites. These materials are often denser than wood, and have the advantages that: they are waterproof; they do not warp; and they can be specifically designed for the strength, density, flexibility, taper, and balance required. Modern police batons are often made of very strong plastics, which are highly resistant to impact. Those materials, however, are often too heavy for a practical walking stick.

Straightness, Finish, and Warping

Some instructors in Asian styles claim that a finish should never be put on any wooden stick weapon, that they should be allowed to acquire a natural finish from the oils of the user's hands over the years. This sounds good, but it virtually guarantees that the shaft will warp. For proper use, the walking stick shaft must be straight. If it warps, it is useless.

If not properly dried, and sometimes even if it is, an unfinished piece of wood will continue to lose moisture in dry surroundings. Wood is not homogeneous, and most woods do not have isotropic properties. What that means is that, as a wood shaft loses moisture, the wood fibers at different places in the shaft shrink at different rates and the shaft bends. Permanently. Imported woods, and especially tropical woods, are rarely dried to the correct moisture content for the conditions of storage and use that they will encounter in North America, so they warp during the winter in any house with central heating in the northern United States and Canada, and at any season in the drier parts of the American Southwest.

A walking stick must have a good finish to keep it from warping and the best is hand-rubbed with boiled or raw linseed oil finish, similar to the finish applied to fine gunstocks. This finish not only protects the wood from warping, it is attractive, emphasizing the natural beauty of the wood; it is washable; it is not slippery; it is easily touched up when necessary; it is inexpensive; and it is extremely durable. Its only disadvantage is that it requires time and patience to put on correctly.

Length

The stick should provide comfort and ease when used as a walking stick. The correct length gives a natural air to the walking stick that helps disguise its nature as a potential weapon. It puts people at their ease. Moreover, if you enjoy walking with it, you will. The stick does you no good at all if it is propped in a corner at home when you need it most. As the correct length depends on the size of the person who uses it, each stick must be fitted to its individual owner.

One way to measure the proper length is to stand sideways on a flight of stairs holding the walking stick with the crown of the crook or the top of the knob even with your hip joint and the tip of the walking stick hanging over the edge of the step. Have someone else mark the walking stick even with the bottom of your foot where the shaft hits the top edge of the step. Cut the walking stick there. Depending on the shape of the handle and the "feel" of the walking stick, the length of your walking stick may vary about one-half inch either side of this height.

After the stick has been cut, a good, stout, secure brass or iron ferrule should be fixed to the end with ferrule cement[5] or epoxy. Epoxy holds better, but the ferrule cement allows you to salvage a ferrule from a broken stick. Every walking stick should be purchased over-length with the ferrule separate. Older style ferrules, with an iron peg protruding 1/2 or 3/4 inch from a brass sleeve, are virtually unfindable today. Even commercially made brass ferrules are hard to find, but metal sewing thimbles and sections of old shotgun barrels make satisfactory ferrules. For walking, the ferrule end should be covered with a rubber tip.

Strength and Weight

Your stick is an impact weapon. You hit things with it, and often what you hit may be very hard. A broken walking stick is pretty futile, so you need a strong stick. To a certain extent, the heavier the stick, the stronger; but you also need fast technique, and the heavier a stick, the slower and harder it is to control and beyond a certain point, the less effective as a weapon. Although additional weight increases the terminal impact of the blows and may be compensated for by strength and superior technique, a heavy weapon requires a great deal of training for effective manipulation. Another important consideration is that a heavy stick can be less pleasant to walk with, and you are more apt to leave it at home.

A frequent question affecting weight concerns "loading" or weighting a stick to increase the terminal effect of blows. This was a common practice in the 19th and early 20th centuries, when the head of a wooden stick would be hollowed out and filled with molten lead, turning a useful and versatile implement into a murderous bludgeon. I strongly advise against this practice. First, it is very apt to split your walking stick or weaken it so that it will fracture under use, leaving you defenseless. Second, it unbalances the stick. This can make it difficult to manipulate, render it less useful as a walking stick, and drastically limit the techniques you can use effectively. Third, that is not normally the end to use anyway. Fourth, the practice creates an "offensive" weapon, which can cause legal difficulties. Finally, it is a silly thing to do, as much the same effect may be attained in a more useful, legal, and pleasing manner by attaching a metal knob or handle to the top of the stick, carefully selected to give it an attractive appearance, a good grip, and optimum balance.

Cross-Section and Taper

Most sticks are round in cross-section, but occasionally, a good blackthorn or other stem stick will have an elliptical or slightly flattened cross section. If properly oriented, an oval cross section acts to increase impact and is a superior feature for self-defense. The cross-section of a good turned walking stick will almost always be round with the rings parallel to the long axis and running the entire length of the shaft. If impact takes place on the ends of the rings, the walking stick is less likely to split. A slightly elliptical turned stick is hard to find but superior to a round one, as an oval cross section provides an index for the proper orientation of the wood grain relative to the striking surface.[6] A crook handle on a cane may be used for the same purpose.

Taper affects both balance and the ability to retain the stick. A stick should taper from the pommel to the point. This allows you to strike with much greater speed and impact, and the resulting weight distribution and balance favors rapid recovery and multiple techniques. A stick with this kind of taper is also much harder for an opponent to retain if he grabs it. A tapered stick held close to a heavy pommel maximizes the reach, speed, and impact of one-handed techniques.

For defensive purposes, the ideal walking stick or cane is a tapered stick of selected straight grain, second growth hickory with a knob or pommel handle so weighted as to place the balance about four inches in front of the hand when the bottom of the hand rests against the pommel or base of the knob. The "Walking Stick™" Company, now sadly defunct, made exactly this design, said to have been modeled after the best of the *la canne* patterns. In any event, it is superior to any other design I have encountered.

Marc Tedeschi illustrates how a cane can be used to assist in a take-down.
Photograph courtesy of M. Tedeschi.

FUNDAMENTALS

One-handed striking techniques with the walking stick grasped at, or just below the handle, make the most of the weapon's advantages in reach, impact, and simplicity. These are the core techniques for the walking stick. Nevertheless, the walking stick may be wielded in one or both hands, and both ends and the middle may be used for blocks, strikes, and thrusts. Used as a lever, the stick may be applied to assist locks, trips, take-downs, and restraining holds; but in spite of this potential versatility, the walking stick is basically an impact weapon, and for maximum effect you strike with the last two to six inches of the far end. The further toward the tip you strike the target, the more easily you will be able to recover and return to a guard position.

The handle's major aggressive use is for "short end" jabbing techniques, with the stick grasped just below the handle. These techniques can be very effective, as the grip allows you to adapt *yawara* techniques for the walking stick.[7] If grasped toward the center of the stick, a really heavy stick or one with a weighted pommel may be used for decisive blows when fighting an attacking animal. This has the possibly fatal disadvantage of reducing distance from fang or claw, so don't miss. The stick should never be grasped at the "point" end for a swinging strike with the pommel. Striking this way with the pommel increases the time necessary to recover from a swing, perhaps fatally so, and puts you at a severe disadvantage if your opponent grabs the stick.

You do not want to begin with a lighter weapon, adopting a heavier one only after attaining strength and skill with the lighter one. It is far better to train occasionally with a heavier weapon than the one you will normally carry. This can give you greater speed and precision when you use your favorite stick. It does, however, have the disadvantage that you are not training with the stick that you might have to use.

Defense Against Dog Attacks

Most self-defense situations with a walking stick will concern loose dogs. A dog is intelligent, very fast, well armed, and he knows where you are weakest. This can be a major problem for an instructor in an empty-hand Asian martial arts style. Those styles have no techniques designed explicitly for use against dogs. Moreover, this subject must be learned mostly from demonstration, lecture, or reading. A dog doesn't know how to fight other than seriously, and on no account may you injure or hurt a canine training partner.

When fighting a dog, you want to keep your stick between you and the dog. If an attack is not serious but merely threatening, you may evade it by merely pointing the stick at the dog using a two-hand grip, as if holding a spear. Shout "no" at the same time, a word every dog knows. Keep your eyes on the dog, but don't stare it down. The dog may back off, or more seriously, circle while growling. If you circle with it, it may decide that you are too much of a threat and back off. If the dog maintains its ground, it may be trying to defend territory. Back away, slowly, from whatever the dog is defending. Never turn away, and never, ever, run.

If the dog grabs the stick in its jaws, don't get into a tug-of-war. If possible, lever the point upward against the roof of the dog's mouth. This is annoying to the dog and it will usually let go. It will then try to bite you. Once the stick is disengaged, move backward and present the point again. Be quick, because the dog will be.

If the attack is serious, never turn your back, never run, and stay on your feet if possible. You will probably have to hurt, injure, or even kill the dog(s) to neutralize the attack. If there are two or more dogs, you are in real trouble. Get indoors if you can, or if you have enough time, climb a tree. Dogs are good jumpers, and if you can't get high enough in time, a large one might pull you out of the tree. Otherwise, get your back to a wall, and project as much menace as you can. I repeat: never turn your back, never run, and stay on your feet if possible.

A dog knows that its front legs are fragile, and will carry its head low to protect them. You have to get past the teeth to get at the legs, and although losing one will slow it down, most dogs are still a threat on three legs. The ribs are also vulnerable, but again, you have to get past the head. So, hit the head. It is your best target because it is closest. A blow across the muzzle or against the end of the nose will incapacitate most dogs, at least briefly. A strong blow on the top of the head will sometimes work, but must often be repeated. Hit very hard.

Defense Against Human Attacks

Individual training is the key. Learn what works for you. Anything else wastes your time.

- "Hit, but don't get hit." In any fighting art, this fencing rule may be considered as Rule 1. It is particularly important when training with an impact weapon as potentially dangerous as a stick.
- Get out of your assailant's line of attack. This is Rule 2.
- Finish the fight as quickly as possible. In an unexpected attack, time is almost never on your side. This is Rule 3.
- In general, the best tactical sequence is to disarm, disable, and disengage.
- Train as much as possible with the stick that you will carry. Sticks vary in

weight, length, balance, and "fit" in the hand; they "feel" different. Training with a different stick may put you at a slight disadvantage, and no disadvantage is good. For the same reason, always train in street clothes.

- Train slowly. All techniques should be first learned in slow motion to ingrain proper "muscle memory" and to permit thoughtful learning and a sense of timing. Slow training enables you to train with a partner, which is vital for understanding the weapon.
- Be aware of the variation in impact force along the trajectory of your weapon. Any long, hand weapon strikes in an arc, and the power of the strike varies with the weapon's position along that arc. Roughly speaking, the power is least at the beginning and end of the uninterrupted strike trajectory.
- Control comes first. Control determines the ease with which you can recover from a strike whether it hits or misses, and your ability to recover puts a limit on the power and speed with which you can strike. If you strike hard with the heavy end, you may have to wait until the end of your stick's trajectory before you can regain sufficient control to perform another technique.
- Stress movement and posture. Only when control, movement, and posture are good should you start training for speed.
- Emphasize speed and timing in both recovery and technique. Timing and speed allow you to deceive a defense and intercept an attack with one of your own. Power comes from speed.
- Sneakiness is always good policy. Most villains tend to regard the cane as an indicator that the person carrying it is handicapped and vulnerable, as may indeed be the case. Carry your cane to reinforce their belief. It makes an effective defense more shocking to the assailant, and may bias any witnesses in your favor, both during the incident and later in court, if it comes to that.

BASICS

Grips

You must be able to grip the stick firmly and swing it rapidly and with control. The single-hand hold should be emphasized. Train both hands, starting with the weak one. A knob-handled or straight cane is held above the pommel. A crook-handled cane is held just above the curve so that the crook provides some protection to your hand. Grip the stick naturally in your fist, as you would an axe or a baseball bat, with the thumb curled down tightly against the fingers. You control the stick with wrist, elbow, and shoulder. Do not grip the stick with a fencing grip, with your thumb extended parallel to the long axis of the stick. The stick is too heavy, most are balanced wrong for control with the fingers, and it is a good way to sprain a thumb.

A stick has two ends, and you have two hands, so you should train with both single- and double-handed grips. A two-hand hold is a strong grip adaptable to several powerful techniques and it enables you to thrust forcefully. Nevertheless, the stick is not a bayonet. A low, two-handed hold deprives you of much of your reach and speed, and your lead hand is an attractive target for a knife or improvised impact weapon. If fighting another person who also has a stick or weapon, the point of your stick should be lower than the handle. When held point upward, a blow with an improvised weapon or knife tends to slide down the shaft of the stick onto the hand.

Your ability to recover from a stroke determines the maximum power that you may safely use in the stroke. A stick striking its target will always rebound to some extent. You have to control this rebound. If you miss, you can improve recovery by changing your wrist angle so that the vector of the point changes and decelerates more rapidly. If you hold a stick toward the point with a heavy pommel at the striking end, recovery may be very slow.

Changing hands and changing grips with the same hand are very important skills. You must be able to change grips rapidly and securely for different techniques and to retain control of the stick if the strong hand is injured. Changing grips or hands in a fight, however, is extremely hazardous as it increases the risk of being disarmed. You might even drop your stick, which is very embarrassing as well as dangerous.

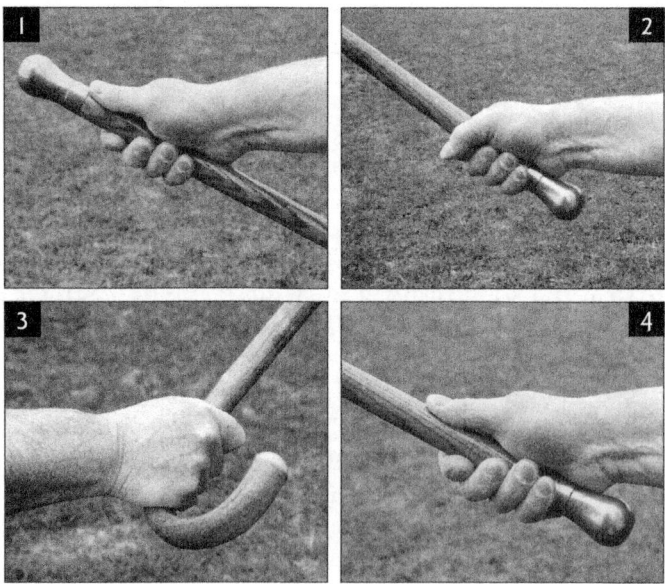

1) The "fencing grip."

2) The "proper" grip for a knobbed (blackthorn) walking stick.

3) The grip for swinging a crook-handled walking stick into a strike.

4) Incorrect fencing grip on the walking stick. Notice the thumb position.

Photographs courtesy of R. Dohrenwend.

The hand holding the stick is not necessarily your most effective hand. The free ("live") hand has to be kept out of the way of an opponent's strike, but it must also be kept in a position where you can use it. It should never be chambered to the side in a fist, as often done in karate, or placed on the rear hip as is customary in saber fencing. It does you no good at all there. The "live" or free hand may be held close to the same side of the chest, brought across the chest (esgrimista style), "ride" on the forearm holding the stick (taiji style), or kept out to one side for balance. Whatever its "default" position, as the term implies, the live hand is not static. You should be able to use it quickly for reinforcing a stick technique or for balance, grabbing, blocking, or striking on its own. You may reinforce your grip by grasping the wrist with the "live" hand. Be alert for opportunities to use that hand.

Mobility and Stances

Martial arts stances may be difficult for someone who habitually carries a walking stick, and some stances may be beyond them altogether. Many people use a walking stick because they can't assume a strong stance. Most martial arts stances are inappropriate even if you are fit; you must avoid static positions, long stances, and low stances entirely. You do not need a strong stance to effectively use a stick; you need mobility and room to move.

You should start facing your potential opponent in a short, relaxed balanced stance, with the stick in your hand, point downward. Do not lean on the stick or put any weight on it. This stance gives you several options for preempting or intercepting an attack. Your first move should be aggressive and decisive. You want to stop the attack immediately, not become involved in a fight; but if you do, circle and side-step, keep moving, and control the tempo of the action. You must never allow a pause while you are within your stick's striking distance. A pause must only be allowed when you move out of range.

Left: Fencing Stance, *tierce* position.
Right: Taiji "toof guard", also called hanging guard.
Illustrations by Jon Parr (www.jonparr.com).

Do not assume a static defensive stance, and avoid the classical fencing *tierce* posture.[8] If you stop and assume that posture as a static defense, the hand holding the stick offers your opponent a very attractive advanced target. The stick is not a sword, and there is no hand guard. A blow to the hand holding the stick can disarm you, and it can badly injure the hand. That stance tends to encourage straight line movement and the lunge attack, and both are quite unsuited to the defensive use of the walking stick. If you are defending against a canine attack, you may assume the fencer's *seconde* position, a stance with the hand holding the cane in front of you. That hand should be higher than the point, as you have to keep the point directed toward the dog's face.

It is better to fight from a short back stance with your unarmed side forward. If you are right handed, the best position is a right hand, hanging guard with the left foot advanced, which allows a greater variety of moves. The hand holding the stick should always be higher than the stick point. This stance provides maximum protection to head and hand, offers good balance, and allows an attack on "the pass," where the rear foot passes the front foot and the moving body puts more force into the strike.

Do not raise your feet any further than necessary to step over an obstacle. If you have to carry a walking stick, your stance and balance aren't that good anyway. The last thing you need is to raise one leg like a prancing horse while trying to balance on the other. Step low. Keep the feet near or on the ground. Move with the knees bent and with unequal weight distribution for speed of movement within the context of the natural stance, modified back stance, walking stance, and "T"-stance. Only if you are not handicapped and your balance is good should you withdraw a leg from an attack by lifting that leg.

Avoid techniques that require spinning the body. Turning your back on an opponent is rarely a good idea. You always lose sight of him for an instant, giving away too much to an opponent who may be faster than you thought. If you must practice spinning moves, always make sure you use the walking stick to protect both back and head during the spin.

Context and terrain are extremely important. Practice outside on uncertain footing as much as possible. A handicapped person must train with the walking aide that he will normally carry, and must learn to use context, finding support against furniture, walls, railings, etc., and to use every terrain feature to his best advantage. This is more important for him than for a person who can fight out of a normal stance. If his walking stick must be used as a weapon, a handicapped person is unlikely to be able to strike from a strong stance, and he becomes increasingly unstable the longer he is deprived of the stick's support.

Defensive Basics

You are not training for competition, and stick fighting is not fencing. Your chances of encountering a fencer with a stick are remote, so don't train to fight against another walking stick. Learn to use your stick against knives, clubs, chains, bottles, and empty-handed assaults, but with the exception of the nunchaku, not against Okinawan weapons (*kobudo*), which you will never see outside the dojo. Tailor your training to the kinds of attacks that you are most likely to encounter. For example, when using a hilted weapon or a long tool as a weapon, most people will strike on a right to left diagonal from above.[9] That tendency allows you to predict the general direction of most armed attacks.

One effective general defense against both threatening dogs and people is the "figure 8." It consists merely of weaving a very fast pattern, resembling a number 8 on its side, with the point of your stick to cover your front and sides. The stick makes a lovely noise as it whips through the air, and it is obvious that intercepting the stick at any point in the pattern will hurt. This technique is much easier and safer with a crook-handled cane. Although possible with a knob-handled cane, your grip is not as secure and the technique requires more practice.

You must get out of your assailant's line of attack. You may move to either side or forward. Forward is usually best when it allows you to intercept the attack at a weak point in the strike trajectory. When you move to evade an attack, normally withdraw at an angle to the original line of that attack. The less movement required to take you out of range of an opponent's attack the better. Learn to adjust distance by shifting weight or by stepping with one foot. The angle of the most effective lateral movement depends on the specific attack and the technique you employ in defense. Generally, the best is a single step at approximately 45° to the line of attack. This allows you to exploit the stick's reach advantage.

Never forget that you do not have a hand guard and that your hand(s) are very vulnerable. The best protection for the hand is to move it out of the way of a blow, so practice moving your stick hand to the rear as rapidly as possible. The hand should move horizontally, the point must be kept below the hand, and the point must be directed at your antagonist throughout the move. Position your stick to deflect the blow at the level targeted by your enemy.

Your opponent shares that hand vulnerability. Stop hits to his thumb, hand, wrist, and forearm are preferred to any block or parry once your antagonist is committed to his attack.[10] A stop thrust to the face is a good technique if your opponent has telegraphed an intention to attack with a long impact weapon and you are inside the trajectory of that weapon. Stop hits against a horizontal strike must angle your hand above the plane of the strike, otherwise the result can be a double hit that might disarm you.

If you are fighting a person who has a weapon, you may use classical fencing parries (deflections). Unlike modern fencing, all parries must be made with force and power. When parrying a stick or improvised impact weapon attack,[11] try to parry close to the point of his weapon. This gives you more effective deflection. Whenever you parry, you should hold your hand higher than your point to allow the assailant's weapon to slide away from your hand. The saber parries in *prime*, *seconde*, *quinte* and reverse *quinte* are very good. Although you can parry in *tierce* and *quarte*, you have to be much more careful. Those parries require more power to keep your hands safe. You may reinforce a parry with your "live" hand, holding that hand flat along one side of the stick.

Once the assailant's weapon has been deflected, it can be a mistake and dangerous to disengage immediately, especially if you are blocking or moving your opponent's weapon from a low hand position, i.e. in *tierce* or *quarte*. By "sticking" to his weapon, you maintain control of the fight and prevent a rapid *riposte*.

A stick is not a blade, so it is more vulnerable to being grabbed by your opponent. Stick releases call for strength and timing, so it is more desirable to avoid a grab than to have to execute a release. Adopting the high guard with the stick held in the reverse hand and attacking on the pass will help prevent grabs but will not eliminate that danger altogether. Emphasizing strikes over thrusts also helps.

If the stick is grabbed, you do not want to struggle for the stick. It is essential to effect a release immediately by an aggressive attack and regain control of your stick. Specifics determine tactics and you have many options, but here are two examples of the kind of technique that might work. If your opponent is facing you and has both hands on the stick, raise the stick sharply, drawing his hands, arms, and attention upward and execute a low front snap kick. If your opponent grabs one end of the stick, grab the stick below his hand with your free hand, and pivot around his hand to execute a horizontal or vertical butt stroke to the head (techniques from bayonet fighting). It is best to step to the outside of his arm, but you may have to step in instead.

Offensive Basics

With a human antagonist, try to establish immediate control of the situation. If you can escape a bad situation without recourse to your weapon, do so. Never threaten with your weapon or engage in preliminary ritual with your antagonist.

Although the whole point of successful self-defense is escape, you need offensive techniques because you have to hit into your opponent's attack, preempt it, and neutralize him. As soon as you decide you are under attack, use your weapon. The odds for survival increase if you can get in the first blow and disable or disarm your assailant, so your best response is to step to the outside of the attacking arm and strike it hard.

The side-step will break your opponent's momentum and bring his advanced targets into range. The hand is the best target, followed by the wrist, the "mound" on the forearm, and the elbow. If you get a good opportunity to attack an advanced leg: the knee, the calf of the leg, and the Achilles tendon are good, incapacitating targets. Let the stick "glance" or rebound after it hits, so that you can strike another target as quickly as possible, changing attack levels and directions. You have to end the fight in your favor as quickly as possible.

Divide body targets into four categories: 1) hard, 2) soft [a good rule of thumb is to strike to the hard and thrust to the soft], 3) advanced/extended, and 4) core targets.

- **Advanced**: The stick gives you an impressive advantage of reach over an assailant who is unarmed or who has a knife, so stress reach and train to strike specific targets on an extended arm, hand, or leg.

- **Core**: This is where the thrust is most useful. Learn a small number of very specific targets that will neutralize an assailant quickly and decisively, even if that assailant is in one of the DDD states (drunk, drugged, or deranged) or armed.

If you cannot get outside your opponent's attacking radius, intercept or preempt the attack by stepping in. Parry, block, or stop hit the blow before it can develop; or strike or thrust immediately into a core target. The collar bone is a good core target, as it requires only 16 pounds of force to break. If the attacker is wearing heavy outdoor clothes, a thrust to the eyes or throat can be especially effective. A strike to the side of the head will often end an attack quickly. A "short end" thrust into the abdomen is also effective.

Although a rapid sequence of uninterrupted blows delivered as rapidly as possible to as many targets as possible, especially the advanced targets and head, may overwhelm your assailant's sensory capacity, confuse him, and provide an opening for a decisive blow, this is only possible if you are fit and have a balanced weapon that permits good stick control. It is better to concentrate on short, quick combinations of three or four techniques.

In any event, you have to control your stick at all times, so you must learn to handle impact; strike glancing blows; control rebound; and rapidly switch to an alternate level, target, or opponent. You need something that you can strike in training. A heavy bag is good, and you can make a satisfactory one out of an old barracks bag filled with rags. It is very tough and more resistant to stick impacts than most commercial bags. It is also cheap. You can make a very useful training dummy out of three small tires and a nylon rope. "Cookie" type spares or small trailer tires work best. Hang them from a rafter or tree branch, one under the other, so that they can swing freely, much like a child's swing. The tires have enough inertia so that you don't have to tether them, they give you realistic impact and rebound, and they are elastic enough to protect your stick.

Training dummy made out of three old tires and a length of nylon rope.

Photography courtesy of R. Dohrenwend.

A hanging piece of two-inch manila rope also makes a good target, and a tennis ball hanging on a string provides good practice for speed and dexterity. A Mason jar gasket hanging on a string is useful for learning point control for thrusts, especially if you have a number of them at various heights, and allow them to swing. As you progress, use smaller and smaller rings.

Avoid strength techniques involving hooking, holding, or takedowns, they are tactically unsound and irrational. You are not trying to capture someone; you are trying to injure him so that you can hobble off faster than he can. I am reminded of an elderly lady who was visiting a farm and was somewhat nervous of a large aggressive gander. She was told that if the gander attacked, she should grab his neck behind the head and the bird would be helpless. One morning, crossing the yard, the gander attacked her, and she did as she was told. Unfortunately, the grass was wet with dew and slippery, and she fell on her back. Unhurt, but still clutching the increasingly annoyed bird, she did not dare let go of him to get up again. She needed help to release him and get back onto her feet.

That goose weighed no more than 20 pounds, if that. Imagine this lady attempting to hold or take down a 200-lb human assailant. Unlikely, but even if successful, she would be in a pickle. She cannot let him go and, over the long run, she cannot hold him. If you have to carry a stick, you are probably not very strong and presenting the crook of a curved handled stick makes it too easy for an assailant to disarm you. You are not a police officer and you are not trying to subdue and capture your assailant. You just want to neutralize him so that you can escape uninjured. Your health and safety is always a much higher priority than your assailant's.

Suggested Basic Syllabus

- Proper grip and ready/guard positions
- Targets for strikes and thrusts, against both canine and human opponents
- Covering: the "figure 8" and clearing sweeps
- One-handed hits: snaps and whips
- Thrusts
- Evasions and "stop" thrusts and hits
- Deflections, parries and blocks
- Close quarter: "short end" and two-handed techniques
- Grab releases
- Supplementary techniques (all close-range)

Always remember, the walking stick is basically an impact weapon.

SIDE BAR 1: The Sword Cane

I wish to state categorically that the walking stick is a superior weapon to the sword cane. The sword cane is merely a curiosity, and even in the hands of an experienced fencer, it is useful only if a) it is extremely well made and thus expensive; b) it has sharp edges as well as a point; and c) your opponent is inexperienced or untrained.

There are several reasons for these statements: First, the stick is faster to get into action than the sword cane. Second, you lose the versatility of technique possible with a strong stick. Third, a sword cane is noisy. The blade rattles loosely within the shaft that forms its scabbard. This is inescapable if the handle of the cane must be rotated to free the blade. Fourth, the hollow shaft is usually weak, which reduces the utility of the sword cane as a support and as a weapon. Fifth, most sword cane blades are pointed with no edges. They are thrusting weapons that can be grabbed and held, and once an enemy is past the point, all your sword cane does is to put one of your hands, usually the strong one, out of action.[12] Sixth, if you have to use a sword cane, it gives you no choice but to inflict grievous bodily harm on your attacker. Finally, in most jurisdictions, the mere possession of a sword stick will probably cause you severe and disagreeable legal problems (a possible felony).

SIDE BAR 2: The Umbrella

Generally, the umbrella is an emergency weapon of limited utility. The umbrella is easier for your opponent to parry, and easier to grab than a stick. The umbrella shank is usually weak and the folded cloth material acts as padding, so strikes with the umbrella are relatively ineffective. The umbrella may only be used as a point weapon. It commonly has a long narrow ferrule that may be thrust, like a foil, at your opponent's face, in which case it is extremely dangerous. The handles on umbrellas, however, are commonly ill-shaped and too weak for this to be a good move unless you take your opponent by surprise. Of course, a folding umbrella is almost completely worthless as a weapon.

This effectively limits most of your techniques to two-handed blocks and thrusts. You grip the umbrella at the handle and about a foot back from the point. This allows you to thrust as with a bayonet and even to use a modified "butt stroke." You can also parry or block effectively as the folds of material and the springy ribs absorb much of the force in blows against the side of the umbrella. Unfortunately, even with a solid two-hand hold, parrying or blocking an attack may easily bend the shank of the umbrella to the point where it is worthless for continued defense.

If the umbrella is what you carry, however, learn to use it for the most effective defense possible. If you anticipate using an umbrella for this purpose, it should be very sturdy. Opening one suddenly in a dog's face may provide a few seconds grace against the attacking animal.

Conclusions

The question: "why do we train in the fighting arts?" usually has a very large number of answers, but training with the walking stick brings us back to basics. Effective self-defense is really the only valid reason. There is no Zen or Dao connection, no use in sports, no performance value, and little purpose as an exercise for weight loss or fitness. We train with the walking stick because age, injury, or disability has reduced our fighting capability and we have a need for an effective defense against personal attack. Perhaps more than for any other defensive weapon, walking stick instruction must be tailored to the individual's needs and physical abilities.

When training in this or any fighting art for serious use, it is essential to train with basic, fast, safe or secure, simple, and strong technique. This is what you will use in an emergency. Avoid sophisticated, slow, elaborate, risky, and weak techniques. You will not remember or properly perform them under stress anyway. Given the cane's advantages as a defense for the disabled or solitary, useful exercises should be designed for low maintenance and solo training, and should always match the characteristics of the stick favored by the student. Practical basics with the walking stick can be acquired very rapidly, and the idea is to become an adequately skilled fighter in a short time. After a minimum amount of formal instruction, you should be able to train, maintain, and even improve your skills on your own, and you want to reach this goal as rapidly as possible.

There are generally two kinds of people who wish to learn defensive techniques with the walking stick: the injured or handicapped who need to use a cane for support, and the fit who carry a walking stick to enhance the pleasure and safety of a walk. The handicapped person needs a first strike capability, and good timing and speed are essential. He may get only one chance. He may be terribly vulnerable because of age, a physical defect, or infirmity and may be unable to block or deflect a determined attack. There may be no first strike in karate, but this philosophy is a luxury the handicapped under threat cannot afford. He must hit into the attack and discourage his assailant immediately. He cannot easily escape a nasty situation, so he has to disable his assailant(s) for safety, inflicting greater damage for effective defense than a fit, healthy person in a similar situation.

Although the walking stick can provide very effective self-defense against an attack by a single dog or man, you must recognize that a man with a cane facing an armed man; multiple assailants; or a large, angry, or trained dog is under an immediate and potentially lethal threat. In those circumstances, a police officer, who is often better trained with his baton than you are with your cane, and who has far more experience in violent confrontations than you, will almost invariably prefer his hand gun. In addition, the modern officer usually has a partner and a radio to call for back-up, and he may be wearing Kevlar body armor. You have none of these advantages. Think about that, and be cautious about inflated claims for a walking stick's effectiveness.

We select the walking stick to counter a low probability hazard of an assault of moderate severity. If the hazard were lethal in nature and our chances of encountering it were moderate to high, we would carry a firearm as well as, or instead of the walking stick. For example, if you were to encounter a vicious dog on a country road, a stick would probably save you. But if you ran into a loose bull or a cranky bear, it probably would not. You are far more likely to encounter the dog, so the stick is a reasonable choice.

There is a lot of flexibility and variety possible with the walking stick that makes its study very interesting indeed. The walking stick or cane can be a very versatile weapon with the potential for a wide variety of complex techniques that could easily earn it status as an independent martial art. Nevertheless, it is a very simple weapon, and effective defense with the cane is easily and quickly learned. Most of its value is to be found in this simplicity and the rapidity with which genuine defensive capability may be acquired. The fact that there is very little competent instruction available for this weapon offers both a challenge and an opportunity to the thoughtful martial arts instructor.

SIDE BAR 3: Cane Vocabulary

ENGLISH	GERMAN	FRENCH	SPANISH
cane or walking stick	*spazierstock*	*canne*	*baston*
handle (head)	*griff*	*pommeau, poignee*	*mango*
knob	*knauf* or *knopf*	*pommeau, bouton*	*pomo*
crutch	*kruecke*		
crooked	*rundhaken*	*courbe*	
crown			
outside line			
inside line			
heel			
mouth			
nose			
band, collar (ferrule)	*rIng, band*	*bague* or *virole*	*anillo*
eyelet			
wristcord			
shaft or shan	*schuss*	*jonc* or *fût*	*vara*
shank peg			
ferrule, tip, finial	*zwinge* or *absatz*		*contera*

Notes

[1] In modern English, the terms now vary slightly in meaning between the United Kingdom and North America. In Britain, a cane is a slender, tapered stick usually with a knob handle, an elegant dress accessory; while a "walking stick" usually refers to the crook-handled walking aid. In the United States, the meanings are reversed. In fact, although this seems to reflect current usage,

either term is correct for any stick used as a walking aid. For convenience, we will use "walking stick," "cane" or "stick" interchangeably throughout to apply to both crook- and knob-handled walking sticks.

[2] One modern suggestion for the origin of the word "cane" comes from the use of that word for Malacca *rattan* (Mandarin: *teng* or *shu*). The word "cane" in commerce refers to rattans that are 2cm or greater in diameter, and 9 foot lengths of these "canes" are sold in bundles to walking stick and cane makers.

[3] Including the knob, the crook, the crutch, the opera, the "T," the "L" or cross hook, the pistol grip, the straight handle, the hunting hook, and the rare "*bec de corbin*" ("crow's beak," a short curved hook).

[4] For more detailed information on wood properties and suitability, the reader is referred to the standard works on woods and impact tools listed in the bibliography. This information is extremely useful for evaluating the woods used in the construction of walking sticks.

[5] Obtainable from any archery supply house.

[6] One of the first things that a boy was taught in baseball is "Don't hit the ball with the label side of the bat."

[7] The *yawara* is a 6-inch stick, adaptable to a variety of techniques, but often used for short jabbing blows to enhance blows to pressure points.

[8] A classic fencing term referring to one of the five basic saber parries: first (*prime*), second (*seconde*), third (*tierce*), fourth (*quarte*), and fifth (*quinte*). These parries roughly follow the sequence from drawing the saber to assuming the *en garde* position at *tierce*. *Quarte* is a parry to the left at the same level as *tierce*, and *quinte* is a head parry. The hand is held high with the point slanting downward in *prime*, *seconde*, and *quinte*. It is held low with the point upward toward the opponent's face in *tierce* and *quarte*.

[9] This observation led to the development of the U.S. Navy "boarding caps," first issued around 1803 during the Barbary Wars. These caps offered very effective protection from cutlasses when boarding an enemy vessel.

[10] A fencing term for a preemptive strike to your opponent's hand or forearm, intercepting his attack. A "stop thrust" is a preemptive thrust to any vulnerable core target: the face, throat, or abdomen.

[11] Pipe, shovel, axe, rake, pick handle, baseball bat, hoe, broom, wrench, hammer, etc.

[12] A rapier fighter fought with both dagger and rapier for a reason.

Bibliography

Allanson-Winn, R., & C. Phillipps-Wolley. (1890). *Broadsword and singlestick*. London: George Bell & Sons.

Baltazzi, E. (1983). *Stick fighting: A practical guide for self-protection*. Rutland, VT: Charles E. Tuttle Co.

Barton-Wright, E. (1901, January). "Self-defense with a walking stick." *Pearson's Magazine*, 11, 11–20. Reprinted at http://ejmas.com/jnc/jncart_barton-wright_0200.htm.

Barton-Wright, E. (1901, February). "Self-defense with a walking stick." *Pearson's Magazine*, 11, 130–139. Reprinted at http://ejmas.com/jnc/jncart_barton-wright_0400.htm.

Burtscher, W. (1945). *The romance behind walking canes*. Philadelphia: Dorrance & Co.

Coleman, D. (1966). *Woodworking factbook*. New York: Robert Speller & Sons.

Department of the Army (1992). *Combatives: Field manual, 21–150*. Washington, DC.

Dike, C. (1990). *Walking sticks*. Princes Risborough: Shire Publications, Ltd.

Echanis, M. (1978). *Basic stick fighting for combat*. Burbank, CA: Ohara Publications.

Evangelista, N. (1998). *Fighting with sticks*. Port Townsend, WA: Loompanics Unlimited.

Goss, J. (2003). *Hanbo: The aiki way*. Baltimore, MD: Imaginator Press.

Grant, D. & Hart, E. (1983). *Shepherd's crooks and walking sticks*. Clapham: Dalesman Books.

Hatsumi, M., & Chambers, Q. (1971). *Stick fighting: Techniques of self defense*. Tokyo: Kodansha.

Hurley, J. (2001). *Irish gangs and stick fighting in the works of William Carleton*. Philadelphia: Xlibris.

Hutton, A. (1901). *The sword and the centuries or old sword days and old sword ways*. London: Grant Richards.

Jones, A., & George, C. (1999). *Stickmaking handbook*. Lewes, UK: Guild of Master Craftsmen.

Kaufman, S. (2000). *Zen and the art of stick fighting*. Chicago: Contemporary Books.

Klever, U. (1996). *Walking sticks*. Atglen, PA: Schiffer.

Lang, H. (1923). *The walking method of self-defense by "an officer of the Indian police."* London: Athletic Publications. (Boulder CO: Paladin Press, 2004 reprint).

Monek, F. (1995). *Canes through the ages*. Atglen, PA: Schiffer.

Myung, K. (1988). *The cane: Techniques. Hapkido weapons Vol. II*. Los Angeles, CA: World Hapkido Federation.

Nardi, T. (1997, Sept./Oct.). "England's stick assault." *World of Martial Arts*.

Panshin, A., De Zeeuw, C., & H. Brown. (1964). *Textbook of wood technology*.

New York: McGraw-Hill.

Record, S., & Hess, R. (1943). *Timbers of the new world*. New Haven, CT: Yale University Press.

Stein, K. (1974). *Canes & walking sticks*. York, PA: Liberty Cap Books.

Styers, J. (1952). *Cold steel*. Quantico, VA: Leatherneck Association. (Boulder CO: Paladin Press, 1979 reprint).

Tegner, B. (1961). *Stick-fighting for self-defense*. Ventura, CA: Thor Publishing.

Tegner, B. (1972). *Stick-fighting: Self-defense*. Ventura, CA: Thor Publishing.

Waite, J. (1880). *Lessons in sabre, singlestick, sabre & bayonet, and sword feats*. London: Weldon & Co.

Wallace, G. (1972). *Stick fighting for self defense*. Los Angeles: Walmac Books.

Whitmore, T. (1973). *Palms of Malaya*. London: Oxford University Press.

U.S. Department of Agriculture. (1955). *Wood handbook, Handbook No. 72*, 528p.

Audiovisual Media

Gilman, M. (2003). *Partner cane*. Port Townsend, WA: Gilman Studio. [VHS and DVD]. (Available from Gilman Studio, 913 L Street, Port Townsend, WA 98368; www.gilmanstudio.com)

Thompson, L. (2004). *Stun, stagger, stop*. Ventura, CA: Cold Steel, Inc. [DVD]. (Available from Cold Steel, Inc., 3036-A Seaborg Avenue, Ventura, CA 93003; www.coldsteel.com)

Acknowledgments

As in every writing of this general nature, the author stands on the shoulders on bigger and better men to get a good view, and I am especially grateful for the very generous contributions by Marc Tedeschi and Michael Gilman, two fine instructors. I would also like to thank Joe Svinth. Only the inevitable errors of fact or interpretation are mine and mine alone.

The Spear:
An Effective Weapon Since Antiquity

"Neanderthal Man Defending His Family from a Wolf Pack"
Painting by Charles R. Knight (1874–1953).
©Rhoda Knight Kalt • www.charlesrknight.com

Introduction

The spear may be man's oldest purpose-made weapon. It goes far, far back into the past, before man really had become man, and it dominated hunting and ruled the field of battle for most of human history and prehistory. The spear is thus of enormous significance for our understanding of human biological, social, and cultural evolution. The term "spear" may be applied to two separate weapons, the throwing spear and the thrusting spear. Although the origins of the two are interrelated, their histories, development, and characteristics are very different.

The bladed thrusting spear is the most effective hand-held, edged weapon of all time. It originated as a weapon for personal protection against wild animals, and it was the first individual weapon which allowed man to confront a dangerous predator with at least some hope of survival. When describing the thrusting spear and the fighting techniques that developed for its use, we must never forget that it is the *only* martial art deliberately developed to fight species other than our own.

In general terms, proper use of the thrusting spear is the oldest and most fundamental human fighting art and more effective in warfare than any other non-projectile weapon. It retained its importance and prestige well into the firearms era, and even today, most armies still issue a bayonet, so that soldiers may convert modern assault rifles into short, clumsy vestiges of this once splendid weapon.

Characteristics

What makes the spear so formidable a weapon? In three words: reach, lethality, and simplicity. Reach and lethality are obvious, but its simplicity is deceptive, and a little thought will quickly show that there is more to it than you might think. To describe a spear, we need to specify its total weight, total length, length of the blade, width of the blade, attachment to shaft, balance point on the shaft, diameter of the shaft, blade material, shaft material, design and material of the crossbar (if present), and design and material of the butt cap (if present).

The spear head is the most important part of the spear. It provides lethality. The thrusting spear kills most reliably by hemorrhage, so it should possess a blade with sharp cutting edges. For most of the spear's history, materials for such blades were unattainable with existing technology. Early spears possessed conical points of organic materials, including bone, antler, firehardened points carved on the end of the shaft, and possibly even animal teeth and ivory. These points killed by penetration to a vital area, and the disturbance of that vital area's function. They were not reliable for a quick kill, and so could be used only for throwing at prey or finishing helpless prey either in a trap or after running it to exhaustion.

Cutting blades were first possible with the appearance of sophisticated lithic technology, and two approaches were effective: edged points and microliths. Other edged spears have been made with shark's teeth. These new spears had the disadvantage that large predators can be very heavy, much stronger than any human, and they have far more stamina, even when badly wounded. To reliably fight and kill a dangerous animal with a spear, the blade has to be wide, strong, and sharp. Such blades were beyond lithic technology, and it was not until Bronze Age metallurgy appeared that a true fighting spear for dangerous animals became possible.

The shaft is as important as the blade, as it provides the spear's reach. It has to take the weight of the animal and keep it away from the man holding the spear. The shaft must be very thick, strong, and resilient. Unfortunately, that also means it must be heavy. Bamboo and rattan have made good spear shafts, but by far the most common material has been wood, and almost everywhere it grows, ash (*Fraxinus spp.*) has been found to supply the best wood for the purpose.

A desperate, dying animal may charge right up the spear shaft, impaling itself to get at the man behind the spear. There has to be a stop or barrier of some sort behind the blade to prevent this, and the obvious solution was the cross-bar. This bar is sometimes integral to the socket or even the base of the blade itself. I am aware of no evidence to suggest that these features—broad blades, heavy shafts, socket attachment, or crossbars—were present on any spears before the development of Bronze Age metallurgy.

The attachment of the spear head to the shaft is extremely important. Basically, there are two methods, the tang and the socket. The simple tang is a weak attachment. It varies in length, depending on the culture, and has to be inserted in a hole in the shaft. Any heavy impact drives the base of the tanged point back against the shaft, and may split it unless the end of the shaft is reinforced, usually by a metal sleeve. To prevent the tanged point from working loose from its wooden shaft, it must be held by one or more retaining pins, which further weakens the shaft.

The socket is a stronger system, as it transfers the force of impact over the entire cross-sectional area of the shaft. The best attachment system combines socket and tang, with the base of the blade broadened into a short cap which fits over the end of the spear shaft to distribute the force of the thrust to the entire end of the shaft. The shaft is then reinforced by metal bands at the points where pins retain the tang in the shaft, or by languets, metal straps which run down the shaft of the spear from the rim of the socket. Languets also protect the shaft from a cutting blow by a sword or axe.

Note the crossbar on this 10th century
Frankish winged spearhead (unknown provenance).
Photograph courtesy of William R. Short.
www.hurstwic.org

The Origin and Development of the Spear

How old is the spear? Carleton Coon (1971: 74) claimed circa 250,000 years for the age of the spear, and a fairly complete spear made from yew (*Taxus* spp.) dating from 115,000 to 125,000 BCE was found inside a straight-tusked elephant (*Elphus antiquus*) skeleton at Lehringen, Germany in 1948. However, a 1995 discovery at Schoningen, Germany (about 60 miles East of Hannover) has pushed this age back to circa 400,000 years BCE (Thieme, 1997).[1] Three complete wooden throwing spears about 2 m long were found, each carved from a single spruce (*Picea* spp.) sapling with broad pointed heads in the densest wood closest to the roots, and with more slender and tapered tail ends. They were heavy weapons, indicating that the people who threw them were strong and practiced.

These spears were found in an archeological context that indicates that they were used for hunting horses. They were also found in connection with a possible hearth. These are the oldest hunting weapons ever found, and along with their context plainly show that the people who used them could think, plan, cooperate, and most probably had a spoken language.[2] Cultural adaptations had become important to this species' survival. The find at Schoningen may confirm a possible spear tip of approximately the same age found at Clacton, England in 1911.

The current explanation of human origins suggests that man evolved in a savannah, a rather open grassland biome, but the data which support that model are heavily biased.[3] These data come from point samples which to date have been determined more by excavation opportunity and taphonomic[4] considerations than by early human distribution.

For most of the history of our genus *Homo*, man was not a formidable hunter, but rather easy and obvious prey. He can't run fast, can't fight, can't dig fast or hide well, and he's delicious. Sort of a large mouse. But unlike the mouse, man can't eat grass. His dentition and digestive system are unable to process the most common foods readily available on a savannah. These characteristics are particularly unadaptive in open areas populated by large predators and fleet footed grazers. So, it is likely that the savannah hypothesis is wrong.

As a plausible alternative, I suggest that modern man evolved and spread as a semi-aquatic primate in riparian habitat, in gallery forests along river banks, and along lake shores and sea coasts. These are complex habitats with reliable food supplies and diverse opportunities for evasion and shelter.[5] Their occupation would allow early man to successfully feed, breed, and evade predation. It is very useful to stipulate these riparian habitats for human origins when we examine the importance of the spear in deep antiquity, and trace its subsequent development and use. If we accept that man, however defined, has been a quasi-aquatic primate occupying riparian or littoral habitat[6] for much of his existence, the first spears were very likely pointed sticks used for gathering food otherwise out of reach, an expansion of their use as digging tools, perhaps for shellfish along a seacoast. I suggest that the spear was originally an aquatic hunting or fishing tool, and that this is a more plausible origin than as a weapon for strictly terrestrial hunting.

To quote Stuart Kauffman (2006: 44), "every feature of an organism, in addition to its obvious functional characteristics, has others that could become useful in totally novel ways under the right circumstances." Early man's riparian habitat forced him to evolve in certain ways which permitted him to move away from that habitat into a new and productive niche. The first species of man to move into tropical grasslands took his fishing sticks with him. Those sticks gradually developed into throwing sticks and hand-held thrusting spears, really no more than pointed sticks, but the oldest terrestrial hunting weapon known. I suggest that early man evolved from a riparian forager with a fishing stick to become a diurnal cursorial predator with a spear.[7]

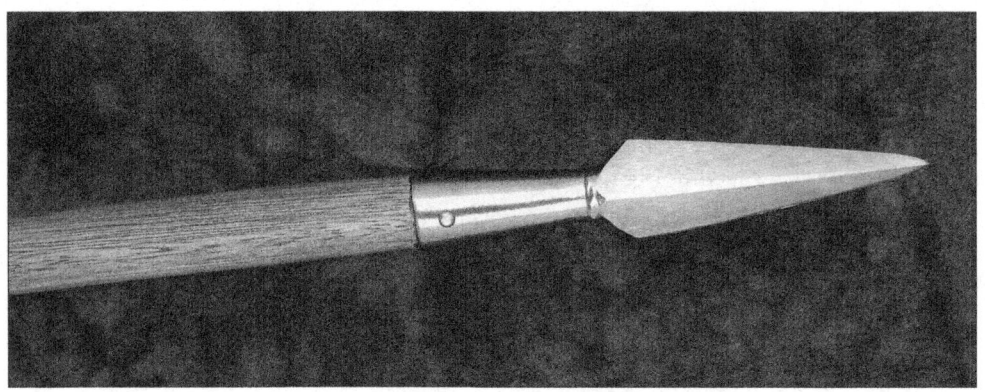

Javelin spear head. Reproduction of a classic form excavated from the Baltic region dating to the 11th century. *Photograph courtesy of Arms & Armor, Inc. www.armor.com*

Although man can't run very fast, he can run considerable distances, and over time a human runner can run a horse or other grazer to exhaustion. At the end of such a chase, the human hunter dispatches his prey at close range with a spear thrust. This strategy, termed "persistence hunting," depends on human physiological adaptations to hot climates which give man a decisive endurance advantage in these long runs.[8] This hunting strategy is rare today, but it may be found among the Bushmen of South Africa and perhaps the Tarahumara Indians of Mexico.

These first thrusting spears were very likely little more than sticks with conical points. Forced to kill at very close range, it soon became obvious that it was better to throw something at a cornered animal than to close with it, so the javelin was born. The thrusting spear was abandoned and reverted to its previous status as a foraging stick.

As persistence hunting requires a hot climate to help exhaust the prey animal, it is not a practical hunting strategy in cold climates. To expand his habitat from the tropics, man had to develop other hunting strategies for cold climate subsistence. I suggest that the limitations of persistence hunting eventually forced ancient peoples to develop strategic hunting technologies, another extremely important step in cultural evolution.

The basic idea behind strategic hunting is to take advantage of seasonal concentrations of animals for migration when they are most vulnerable, and get the most food for the least work. I suggest that throughout its history as a stone-tipped weapon, the thrusting spear was most often used as a specialized lance to deliver a final *coup de grâce* to large grazers immobilized by deep snow, traps, pits, pens, nets, or fire, or held at bay by dogs, or driven by women and children into a blocked canyon or over a cliff (buffalo jumps), where they could be finished off by these lances. Most Arctic peoples combine sea-mammal hunting, fishing, and land hunting, placing emphasis on water resources, which are richer than land resources. Tundra life requires access to marine resources.

The maritime javelin or harpoon would have played a significant, perhaps even a determining, role in the ecological spread of humans along coasts and archipelagos from the tropics into the higher latitudes, areas of more severe climate where vegetable foods were less diverse, less valuable, and less easily attainable, but teeming with oceanic resources. The northern ocean rims are an extremely attractive habitat for a littoral species with the technology to exploit marine mammals. The harpoon was essential for human migrations during the late Quaternary.[9]

Only when lithic technology had advanced to the level that composite microlith points and fluted stone points[10] were made, did a true if fragile thrusting spear reappear. I suggest that this did not occur until late in the Quaternary. The fragility of stone points meant that this new weapon could only be used effectively under very limited circumstances. These new trusting spears were very likely a simple point mounted at the end of a long shaft, a weapon similar to the 19th century whaler's lance, and used for the same purpose, for dispatching larger marine animals, very possibly even the walrus and small whales. The small stone point on a lance, however sharp, had to be directed at a specific organ, usually the heart, which required precise knowledge of its location.

When this marine lance was adapted to kill large grazing animals, mammoths for example, it became the earliest bladed thrusting spear. Such weapons require sharp points, sophisticated lithic technology, to kill effectively. The points must cut. This requirement strengthens our contention that the terrestrial thrusting spear is a much more recent development than the throwing spear, and it is likely that, except for this new role for the marine lance, the stone-pointed spear remained predominantly a throwing weapon. These lances had small points, which allowed them to penetrate a long distance to reach a vital organ. Relatively small points have remained characteristic of lances and pikes throughout the history of the spear, and in general, the longer the spear, the smaller and narrower the point.

The long lance is almost useless as an individual weapon. It is unsuitable for hunting any large game that can still fight back. The weapon is unwieldy, and the point far too small to ensure a crippling wound or a quick kill. Without an effective thrusting spear, individual human hunters were unable to directly confront large, aggressive predators, all too apt to consider the man at the other end of the spear as a tasty snack. Humans would have avoided them as much as possible. The lack of predator remains associated with human artifacts of the Quaternary supports this conclusion.

You have to get very close to your prey in order to properly use a hand-held thrusting spear. The heavy hunting spear for encountering large terrestrial predators and other dangerous game at close range must have a large, strong, slashing blade if it is to be effective. Such blades were not available until the development of crossbar (about 90% copper to 10% tin) metallurgy. The hand-held thrusting spear is a Bronze Age invention. Although tactics varied with the characteristics and behavior of the animal to be killed or driven off, spear hunting techniques are simple and seem to have changed relatively little since the Bronze Age.

The Greeks differentiated clearly between javelins and the heavy thrusting spear, preferring light javelins to the heavy spear for stag hunting. It is known that spears were used to hunt lions in Macedonia about 300 BCE, and Xenophon, in his *Cynegetius*, gives very specific advice for hunting wild boar with the spear. In both the pursuit of dangerous game and in warfare, an archer on foot or in a chariot was always protected by spearmen. This clearly indicates that the importance of combined weapons was understood at an early period.

NEXT PAGE
"Hunters Holding a Manchurian Tiger at Bay."
Painting by Charles R. Knight.
© R. Knight Kalt • www.charlesrknight.com

Spear Head Cross-Sections

Metallurgy made it possible to make spear heads with a wide variety of shapes depending on purpose, appearance, or perhaps even merely whim. Thicknesses vary, and the blades may be provided with grooves, fullers (broad grooves), and ribs both rounded and sharp. Cross-sections usually vary with distance from the point of the spear. The more compact cross-sections are usually found on the heads of throwing spears, while the more extended ones result from the cutting blades provided on a thrusting spear. A few examples are shown:

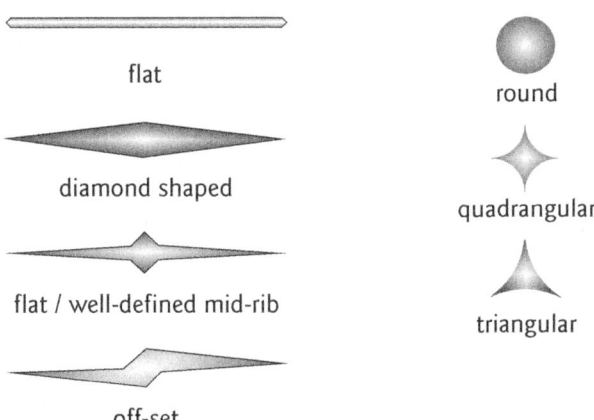

The Romans hunted the boar with barred spears, using a straight underhand two-handed thrust directed at the vital spot between neck and shoulder blade. They also used those spears to hunt leopards. The *bestiaries*, gladiators who fought animals in the arena, also used barred spears.

> ... man was able to inflict an effective wound in a large animal, while at the same time keeping out of range of any retaliatory blow from tooth or claw. At least he was able to do this if the spear did not enter too deep because of the strength or impetus of the animal's charge. ... it will never be known when hunters first realized the advantage of fitting some kind of stop behind the blade to prevent this. – Blackmore, 1971: 82

In the early Middle Ages[11] no special distinction was made in spear design between those used for hunting and those used for war. The most common type during that era had a long narrow blade with a socket to fit over the shaft. There were wings or bars protruding from each side of the socket. This *lanca uncata* or *Flugellanze* was wide-spread in Europe and was the general purpose weapon of the Carolingian period (ca. 740–1000 CE).

The primary Anglo-Saxon weapon was a spear held in one hand, and used with a shield. The iron (steel) spearheads seem to have been relatively long and slender with crude sockets for attachment to the shaft. The socket had a longitudinal split, and was hammered closed on the shaft and then secured by one or two rivets passing through the socket and shaft. Blade cross-section could be either diamond or off-set, and blade shapes varied. The longer heads or blades may have been used for cutting as well as thrusting attacks (Underwood, 1999: 40–41). Barred heads do not seem to have been common on Anglo-Saxon spears, so they were either exclusively war weapons, or they had a loose horn bar or equivalent attached to the head by leather thong bindings when hunting. Their spears had an ash shaft ca. 1.50 to 2.75 m (5 to ca. 9 feet) in length and often a cone-shaped iron ferrule on the butt end of the shaft.

The Viking and other northern warriors prized their spears highly, and used them as part of a tactical mixture with axes and swords. The Viking spear shaft was of ash and was from 1.80 to 3.35 m (6 to 11 feet) long, with the shorter spears being of more recent date. The longer shafts *may* have been used originally for hunting small whales and later adapted to warfare. The spear head was of steel, often leaf shaped, and sometimes had "wings" or "bars" to prevent excessive penetration (Griffith, 1995: 178–179). These later "barred spears" were usually all purpose weapons used for both hunting and war.

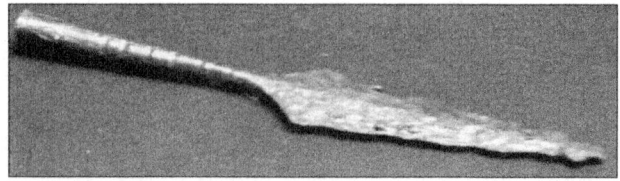

A historic 11th century spearhead. Photograph courtesy of William R. Short. www.hurstwic.org

The fully developed medieval European spear is a staff weapon with a sharp, pointed, heavy, steel head weighing between 0.34 and 0.625 Kg (12 and 22 ounces). The weight of the point is sometimes counterbalanced by a metal butt cap on the other end of the shaft, weighing between 0.226 and 0.453 Kg (8 and 16 ounces). These spears had an average length of 1.80 to 2.45 m (6 to 8 feet), and a total weight of between 1.814 and 2.721 Kg (4 and 6 pounds). The large, sharp blades could rapidly produce massive hemorrhage and were very effective killers.

The crossbar had been simplified, and was no longer an integral part of the socket. It was now a piece of antler, horn, a boar's tusk, or even a small metal bar thrust through the leather straps binding the spear head to the shaft, which made the spear a little lighter and easier to use. This is such a simple and obvious device that it is quite possible that it was known much earlier. Finally, the crossbar developed into a "toggle," a piece of antler, tusk, or horn which was suspended on a thong which passed through a hole in the socket and shaft (Griffith, 1995: 178–179).

In the 14th century, at the end of the Middle Ages, the blade became wider and more triangular, and the wings somewhat larger. Spear designs became more specialized, and the heaviest were those used for bear hunting. Gaston Phoebus shows spear shafts as rough and knobby, doubtless for a better grip (Bise, 1984). At this time, the usual hunting spear was about two meters long, and the blade was usually between 30 and 45cm (12 to 18 inches) (Griffith, 1995: 178–179). Although several new and more elaborate pole arms had evolved from this basic weapon by the 15th century, the older, simpler spear with its crossbar was still in common use for hunting and war. Even as late as the 16th century, the hunting spear was still used unaltered as a military weapon (Blackmore, 1971: 85–86).

The Spear as a Hunting Weapon

The hunting spear with crossbar or toggle has continued in use right up to today. Although other large, dangerous animals can be successfully fought and killed with bladed spears, after the 17th century the spear became gradually restricted in Europe to hunting the European wild boar. In Germany at the beginning of the 21st century, the Puma™ *Saufeder* (boar spear) is still in production, uses the toggle type of bar, and is an expensive weapon.[12]

Heavy bladed spears have to be very sharp, and are very dangerous not only to the animal, but also to the hunter if handled carelessly. A stout leather scabbard should always be firmly laced over the blade for transport. When moving through heavy undergrowth, the hand should be placed just behind the head to better control the blade. A spear has two ends, and a spearman always has to be aware of the "other" end of his weapon. Spears are too long for quick use in heavy cover. If the back end of his spear hits a piece of tough brush and checks his swing while trying to get the blade in line with a charging animal, the spearman is in serious trouble.

Sasha Sieme's book first sparked adventure in 1953.

When discussing spears used for hunting big cats or for protection against attack by aggressive predators, the name of Sasha Siemel, the *tigrero* (jaguar hunter) from Brazil, is the first to come to mind. The *tigre* or Brazilian jaguar (*Panthera onca*) can weigh up to 136 Kg (300 pounds),[13] and Siemel killed more than 30 jaguars single-handedly with the *zagaya* (spear), often alone. If anyone knew how to effectively use a thrusting spear against a large dangerous animal, he did, and we are fortunate that Siemel (1953) wrote about his experiences.

The technique he describes is as follows. The *tigrero* must be able to see the jaguar and have enough room to maneuver and to use his spear, so dogs are used to flush the *tigre* and bring it to bay in an open area. The hunter advances toward the irritated animal holding the spear almost parallel to the ground in both hands. The hunter attempts to provoke the jaguar into a charge by kicking a lump of dirt or sod at its face. If the animal refuses, the hunter thrusts his spear rapidly at the cat's face, then pulls it back and almost immediately thrusts forward again to meet the animal's charge, driving the blade into the neck or chest. Keeping the animal away at the end of his spear, the hunter holds firm until the cat dies. Once impaled on the spear by a charge, the animal may back off the point. If so, it must be provoked into a second charge immediately. The animal may attack in any of several different ways, each requiring different tactics with the spear.

The timing and sureness of the thrust can only be learned in spear fights against those cats, and the odds are not all on the hunter's side. Apparently, a beginner needs a certain amount of luck to survive to become an expert. Confidence and concentration on the part of the spearman are absolutely essential. The concentration, tension, and work of a spear fight with a big cat exhausts the spearman rapidly. The cat is much stronger than the man, so the fight must not last long. A common reaction among spearmen after such a battle is a feeling of weakness and depression, sometimes amounting to sickness, for several days afterwards.

As classical and medieval European sources confirm Siemel's experience, this technique has not varied in any essential for over 2,000 years. According to those sources, a right-handed man is to stand with the left foot forward and the right foot back directly behind the front foot. He wants a very stable stance in the direction he thrusts his spear. The spear is held at waist level with the left hand in front supporting the shaft, while the right hand directs the point and provides the power in the thrust.

The spearman moves forward by moving the spear first and following the spear, stepping first with the left or forward foot. He leans slightly into the thrust at the moment of impact, aiming at a slight angle to the line of the attacking animal. The thrust must be quick. When hunting wild boar, he must watch the boar's head, for the boar can knock the spear from his hands by jerking his head and striking the spear. If he misses his thrust initially, the angle may allow him to strike the animal further back. The spear must have a crossbar, or the animal can run up the spear and kill the hunter. The bar may be fixed or loose; either system works well against boar and bear. After impact, he couches the spear under his armpit for better grip during the fight.

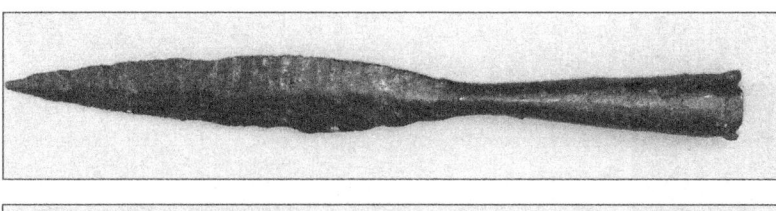

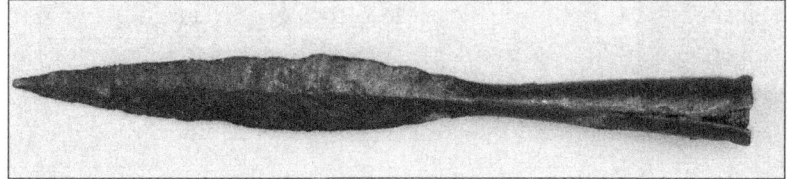

Two sides of an authentic Roman spearhead. *Photograph courtesy of Craig Johnson and the Oakeshott Institute. www.oakeshott.org*

If unable to stand because of dense cover, he may receive a charging animal kneeling on the right knee. The left knee supports the forward hand and the right foot digs into the ground. With this low stance, he may also support the butt of the spear against the ground. As either bear or boar may weigh in excess of 500 pounds, the medieval huntsman was in for an interesting afternoon.

Gaston Phoebus advises that one man should not try to kill a bear with a spear, but that two men may do it with relative safety, if they work together (Bise, 1984). First one man strikes, then the other, each distracting the bear in turn. Nets were also used in combination with spears for taking these animals. The illustrations in his famous *Hunting Book*, all show the thrusting spear used from a low guard position. The thrusting spear is clearly differentiated from the lighter javelin in those illustrations.

In the days before antibiotics and disinfectants, a wound from a large animal, especially a big cat, could often kill through infection. So the shield was developed to keep these animals off and reduce the damage they could inflict until either the spear could be brought back into play or other humans could drive the animal off. Greek lion hunters carried large shields which could be slung from the shoulder, leaving both hands free for an underhand thrust against the beast.

Years ago while bow hunting on the Ottawa National Forest in Michigan's Upper Peninsula, we met some men who were hunting the American black bear with dogs. Unlike most such hunters at the time, these men followed their hounds on horseback. When the bear treed or made his stand, the hunters closed in, and one of their number killed the bear with a spear. We expressed suitable awe, for the black bear in that area is a large animal, but we were told that the animals died very quickly and that there was normally no fight at all after the initial thrust of the spear.

Although the thrusting spear is primarily a hand held weapon, it may be thrown effectively at very close range. Today, a very small number of modern hunters hunt big game, and sometimes dangerous game, by throwing a broad bladed spear a short distance from a tree stand. Sometimes the weapon is even thrust or dropped vertically at the prey. Although the large spear blade causes heavy hemorrhage and a quick kill, the practice is illegal in most of the United States, and it is more of a stunt than anything else. The significant thing for us is that these hunters have found that they must get within 6 to 8 m. (20 to 26 feet) to their intended prey if they are to be sure of a hit (Morris, 2003: 135).

The Spear as a Military Weapon

We may assume that spear techniques in combat evolved from the techniques described above used for fighting dangerous game animals. Although the spear has been known from the late Paleolithic ("Old Stone Age" 2 million years ago to ca. 13,000 BCE) and was known to Neanderthal[14] and Heidelberg[15] man, no evidence of its use against man exists until the final stages of the Paleolithic (Ferrill, 1985: 13 & 16). But of course the spear was eventually used in personal combat against other humans and finally in war, both as a thrusting and as a throwing weapon. With the rise of agricultural and pastoral societies, organized human warfare evolved from strategic tribal hunts, and the spear was adopted as the basic military weapon.

Roman pilum replica provided by CAS Iberia. Overall: 7' 3"
Blade: 31.25" Weight: 3lbs 3oz • *www.casiberia.com*

Hand-thrown spears (javelins) with organic or stone points were almost exclusively hunting weapons in early Europe, used to procure food. They may have been used on occasion as weapons of desperation or opportunity against predators or other humans, but they were not specifically intended to be used as fighting weapons.

When metal bladed heads became available, the javelin was used throughout the ancient world as a short range projectile weapon for hunting, for war, and for sport; it appeared in the Olympic games as early as 708 BCE. Olympic throwers competed for both distance (*ekebolon*) and accuracy (*stohastikon*), but even the distance throws had to be accurate enough to land within a designated target area.[16] For accuracy, the javelin was cast at a round shield from horseback. That game undoubtedly existed before its appearance in the Olympics, possibly going as far back as shortly after the domestication of the horse. Later, throwing the javelin from horseback would be highly regarded as the oldest of Turkish equestrian sports.

In warfare, the javelin reached its highest degree of tactical specialization and sophistication as the Roman *pilum*, designed specifically to reduce the effectiveness of shields. The *pilum* with its characteristic small head and long iron shank, may have been adopted by the Romans from the Scythians, as similar weapons with long iron shanks and barbed heads appear to have been a favored Central Asian weapon at a fairly early period. Later, Germanic and Dacian tribes used a very similar throwing spear, the *angon*, about 210 cm (7 feet) long.

This version of the *angon* was retained into the 12th century in Central Europe, when they gradually disappeared, unable to pierce improved armor. In Iberia, since at least the times of the Visigoths, who seem to have used a variant of the *angon*, the javelin was particularly favored and used by the Spanish peoples into the 15th century at least. According to Froissart in his *Chronicles* (1901), they were very effective.

Although the javelin had essentially vanished from the European battlefield by the 16th century, it was still used there on occasion as a hunting weapon. Henry VIII was a skilled thrower. One of its more specialized uses was in hunting chamoix, and it was prized for this purpose by another of its more illustrious users, Maximilian I of Germany (1493–1519). The weapons (*Scheffline*) were unusually long (2.5 or 2.75 m, or 8 to 9 feet), and required special storage to retain the straightness of their shafts (Cummins, 1988: 95).

In the Middle East, the Turco-Persian javelin (*djerid* or *jarid*) was carried by cavalry in the 17th, 18th and early 19th centuries. These were short weapons, less than a meter in length, with a thin metal or wooden shaft, and a strong, double-edged blade with a pronounced, sharpened mid-rib. They were usually provided with a metal butt cap, they were carried in sets of three in an oblong case suspended from belt or saddle. These short javelins seem to have been reserved for commanders, perhaps more as an insignia than as a weapon, although one source states that they could be thrown with considerable accuracy (Stone, 1934). Some Arab tribes were armed with spears and javelins right up to World War I.

Although the javelin continued in use into modern times, its role was drastically reduced by the bow and it quickly became a relatively rare weapon. The introduction of the bow and arrow offered increased portability, range, impact, accuracy, and firepower, significant advantages over spears for both hunting and warfare. The new weapon sounded the death knell for the older and less effective javelin.

Even so, the Aztecs were using the *atlatl* (spear thrower) and light javelin or dart in warfare in the early 1500s, when Cortez and his small band of conquistadores invaded Mexico, and it was still being made and used as a toy in the Valley of Mexico as recently as the 1940s. This reluctance to abandon the *atlatl*/dart system for the bow and arrow is a powerful argument for the advantages of the earlier weapon.

The bow finally supplanted the *atlatl* as the usual weapon of choice because the bow was more compact, easier to carry, had greater range, greater rapidity of fire, was more powerful, more accurate, quieter, allowed greater stealth, and altogether a superior weapon to the *atlatl*. The *atlatl*'s major advantages are its relative ease of construction, and the larger range of suitable materials for its manufacture.

Unlike the bow and arrow, the *atlatl* and dart, and the javelin, can be used with one arm, leaving the other free for a shield or a close-range, hand-held weapon.

The *atlatl's* widespread use may have retarded the adoption of the bow and arrow in North America. Canadian discoveries have shown that the Arctic Dorset people abandoned the bow when climatic pressure forced them to change their sustenance strategy to hunting marine mammals from shelf ice, reverting to the spear and harpoon (McGhee, 1996: 117, 144). It is interesting that the reversion seems to have provided the Dorset people with a richer and more stable life.

Oddly enough, the *atlatl* and its missile never seem to have been used for war in Europe, the place where this type of spear thrower apparently originated. By the time that metallurgy in the Mediterranean region allowed the fabrication of bronze spear heads, the *atlatl* had disappeared and the bronze headed javelin was propelled by hand alone. I suggest that metallurgy and the domestication of the horse led to the disappearance of the spear thrower in Europe and Asia. The heavier javelin could be used against early shields and armor, against which the *atlatl* dart was relatively ineffective. It was also simpler and faster to use a javelin than an *atlatl* from horseback.

The Short Military Spear

Before describing the historical use of the thrusting spear in military combat, it is instructive to briefly examine the characteristics of the thrusting spear in terms of its use as an *individual* weapon of offense/defense. On foot, the two handed grip on the staff is what gives the spear its speed and versatility. So much attention has been paid to the point of the spear, that modern scholars sometimes forget that it can also be used as a quarter staff, substantially increasing the number of possible offensive and defensive moves. You can bet that warriors using the spear didn't forget this. A simple 6 foot ash or oak staff on its own is a formidable and versatile weapon, and a skilled man with a staff is a match for an expert swordsman. The modern scholar also tends to forget that a bladed spear can be used to slash as well as to thrust. Once again this increases the versatility and utility of the weapon.

Unfortunately, to use the full range of possible spear techniques took up too much room in a front line, where a dense formation for mutual support was tactically necessary. Too much space, and an individual spearman might find himself simultaneously facing several men with spears or with shields and swords. Spearmen also had to fight in dense formations to survive shock attacks by horsemen armed with lances.

By the third millennium BCE, Sumerians were carrying short thrusting spears with metal points (Ferrill, 1985: 42); 18th dynasty Egyptian soldiers were armed with axe, spear and shield (Ferrill, 1985: 49); and the dominance of the spear for over 5,000 years shaped the tactical deployment of ancient armies more than any other weapon (Gabriel & Metz, 1991: 58).

Gabriel and Metz (1991) are among the first to attempt quantitative investigations of the effectiveness of ancient weapons. Although their approach was sound, they were unfamiliar with the weapons they tested. Their study is uncritically accepted and widely quoted, but their results and conclusions are often unreliable. Their figures for the thrusting spear display a remarkable ignorance of the characteristics of this weapon. We can do better.

These authors stated that a one-hand, overhand thrust moves at more than twice the speed of a one-hand underhand thrust. Supposedly, they measured these speeds. But unless you're throwing the thing, you can't accelerate a spear very far in a straight line using an overhand thrust, even committing your entire body to the movement. Try it. Your wrist won't bend far enough, and the spear describes an arc into a futile downward stabbing motion. You've just discarded most of the distance advantage of using a spear. Moreover, your grip on the shaft gets progressively weaker if you try to thrust the weapon overhand in a straight line. It is a very bad idea to weaken your grip on your primary weapon in combat.

Their figure for the impact energy of an underhand thrust (18.3 J or 13.5 ftlb) is absurd. Using more realistic assumptions, it is possible to evaluate the underhand spear thrust's effectiveness (assuming that impact energy is a realistic indicator of effectiveness) at an impact energy of 256 J (189 ftlb). By Gabriel and Metz's estimation, 185 J (137 ftlb) would allow the weapon to penetrate 2mm of bronze armour (their standard), but not iron armour of the same thickness,[17] which they claimed would require 309 J (228 ftlb).

> FTLB = Foot-pound force; a unit of measure for "kinetic energy" equation.
> J = Joule; the joule is a unit of energy, which is defined as the potential to do work.

Recently, however, Bickerstaffe (1999) described an experiment using arrows against replica medieval plate armor, and using his figures and Gabriel and Metz's methodology, we get an impact energy of 136 J (100.5 ftlb), significantly less than the threshold value of 171 J (126 ftlb) for iron armor proposed by Gabriel and Metz. Nevertheless, those arrows smashed through that armor without any problem at all,[18] and in a photograph the armor looked as if it had been under machine gun fire. Gabriel and Metz's conclusion, "...one is left with the impression that against armored troops, the spear was not a terribly effective weapon,..." obviously requires serious reevaluation.

Gabriel and Metz may have been misled by illustrations on surviving Greek pottery depicting spears used overhand. Greek heavy infantry, the *hoplites*, carried a massive, round shield and a long, slender spear, weighing about 1.8 Kg. (4 pounds). The shaft had a small diameter, so that these spears were relatively fragile. As their dense spear/shield formation (*phalanx*) pushed forward before contact, the hoplites carried their spears in an *underhand* thrusting position.

After the shock of contact, if the spear hadn't broken, it was held overhand to jab downward into the mass of the enemy (Hanson, 1989). The possession of a shield in a dense formation imposes this overhand thrust, as you have to stab over the top of a heavy shield, or even two such shields (yours and your opponent's). This explains why Greek warriors are often represented as using their spears with an overhand motion.[19] It is the shield which imposes this otherwise relatively ineffective technique on them, and it is this point in the battle which is depicted on Greek pottery.

The Shield and Spear in Combat

A shield must be strong, light and easy to carry, give good coverage and allow visibility. The heavier the shield, the less useful. Woven wood makes good shields, but leather (rawhide) shields, when properly made, are superior to almost any other material. Leather shields are flexible, light weight, water proof, and effective against sword, spear, and arrow. There are good historical examples.

Buffalo hide from the hump area was used by the Comanches and other tribes of the North American Great Plains, a piece 122 cm (4 feet) in diameter being shrunk until the piece was half the original diameter and at least 2.5 cm thick. These buffalo hide shields were extremely tough; they could deflect a musket ball at fairly close range and they were relatively light weight. Modern experiments (Coles, 1973: 143–147) using cowhide shields show that leather shields were very effective and better than bronze, even when the bronze was reinforced and stiffened with wood. Medieval European leather-covered wooden shields seem to have been heavier, more fragile, less maneuvrable, and harder to make. In general, they were markedly inferior to these "more primitive" leather shields.

Russian spearman with shield.
Courtesy of K. Secours.

Khilton Nongmaithem demonstrating the Thang-ta style of Manipur India.
Courtesy of K. Nongmaithem.

The shields used by the Greeks of classical antiquity were so heavy and unwieldy that they interfered with technique and mobility. These shields were only useful for a rigidly stylized, almost ritual, form of warfare against an identically armed opponent. Their major use seems to have been to cause the spears in the enemy's front ranks to break at the shock of initial contact. As these shields were so heavy, they tired a soldier rapidly and immobilized his left arm. With a broken spear, he had to resort to the *kopis* or short sword—an act of desperation under these conditions.

A skilled warrior with a well-balanced spear would have done extremely well against a swordsman without a shield. But as soon as you factor in shields, things change. The effectiveness of a shield depends upon its characteristics, the weapon used with it, and the strength and skill of the man wielding it. The possession of a shield is a hinderance to a spearman. It limits his technical options, eliminates all two-handed technique, reduces the strength of his thrust, and impedes his ability to use his left arm.

Once the spearman has to carry a shield, he can only use his spear one-handed and one sided. Even with a shield, the underhand thrust is usually the technique used at initial contact—it is harder to block, has greater reach, and would certainly be directed at the unarmored armpit or legs. Low slashing attacks would be particularly effective. But in order to thrust underhand while holding a shield, you must move the shield further around to your side where it provides less protection. In addition, if forced to manipulate the spear with one hand, the spearman has to thrust from the point of balance and to get the maximum reach possible he needs a relatively heavy butt cap to counter balance the weight of the head. He cannot easily shorten grip, and it is much harder to give and recover from swinging blows.

The weapon's point of balance is very important, as it determines how much length is available to the warrior/hunter for a one-handed thrust from behind his shield. If you move your hand behind the point of balance and rest your forearm on the shaft of the spear to hold the point up, you lose speed and maneuverability with the underhand thrust, and it is harder to recover if an opponent knocks the shaft to one side in an attempt to close. You may also "couch" the spear under your armpit to give you additional reach. Unfortunately, you sacrifice much of your flexibility for this increased distance.

After contact, the Greeks often raised their spears and thrust over both shields. When you raise your spear for a one-handed overhand thrust, you expose your right armpit for the duration of the move. This area is highly vulnerable and it is extremely difficult to cover with armor. Ancient armorsmiths didn't even try. Even a blow with the closed fist to this area is dangerous. Ancient warriors certainly knew this. The overhand thrust is also highly visible and easy to deflect and block. The grip is less secure and it is easy for your opponent to deflect the point to one side.

The swordsman doesn't have these problems because of the nature of his weapon, and a shield is much more useful to him when facing a spear. The Roman legions threw their specialized javelins (*pila*), designed to render their enemies' shields useless, and then closed with them to use their fearsome short sword (*gladius*) in combination with a very well-designed shield (*scutum*). Those weapons and tactics made the Romans the most formidable heavy infantry of the ancient world.

The Zulu military genius, Shaka, replaced a light six foot throwing spear with the shorter, stabbing *assagai* with a heavy broad blade and a short staff. This remarkable invention was more a long handled stabbing sword than a spear. Shaka also developed a larger new shield which could be used to hook an opponent's shield, left edges overlapping, and pull that shield away leaving the enemy warrior vulnerable to an armpit thrust. The *assagai* was always used with this cowhide shield with a thrusting underhand motion, similar in some respects to the use of the Roman *gladius*. The incredible discipline and ferocity of the Zulu *impi* (regiments) with these new weapons made them the most formidable foot army in the history of man. In many ways the Zulu *impi* were the tactical equals of the Roman legions, and in others they surpassed them.

A demonstration of a lunge with a spear, showing its reach. *Photograph courtesy of William R. Short. www.hurstwic.org*

SPEAR REPRODUCTIONS

A) **Friedrich IV Spear:** A replica of the hunting spear (*jagdspiessen*) used by Friedrich IV, Duke of Tyrol. This spear style is often called a lug or barred spear. Lugs were used to help control the opponent's weapon. On the hunting spear, they were designed to keep dangerous game from becoming too deeply impaled on the spear. Original: Circa 1430 German, (A32) Innsbruck 1963 (ABB 11). Overall length: 6' 10"; blade: 12" x 4.25"; ash shaft: 6'

B) **12th Century Spear:** The most widely used weapon of the early medieval soldier was the spear. It was an excellent hand-to-hand weapon, having a great advantage in reach over shorter weapons. Spears of this type were in constant use from the early dark ages through the renaissance. The heavy mid-ridge gives this spear superior strength for its weight. Original: 12-14th Century, Spain, Alava Prov. Archaeol Museum, Vitoria. Head length: 11.375" x 3.125"

C) **Viking Spear:** The spear was the basic Viking weapon. They, in fact, had several different types of spears. These, an elongated diamond shape, were effective hand-to-hand weapons. This was the most common use, but these throw well also. Original: 10th century Scandinavian. Head length: 15"

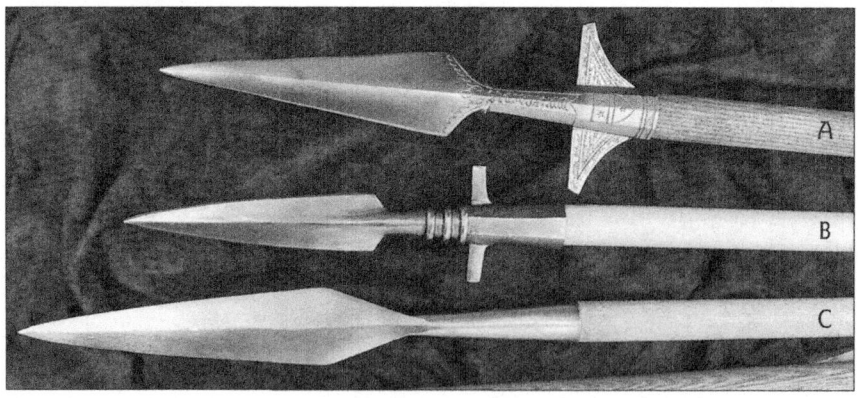

Photograph courtesy of Arms & Armor, Inc. ~ www.armor.com

Sample Defense: When the spearman thrusts, the swordsman deflects the thrust to the outside and controls the spear's shaft with his shield as he closes the distance to attack the spearman. *Photographs courtesy of William R. Short. www.hurstwic.org*

The Horseman's Lance and the Pike

Although a separate weapon, the cavalry lance is a type of thrusting spear and deserves brief mention here, if only because of its antiquity and because it led to the development of the pike. The lance is longer than a normal spear, as a horseman requires a longer reach. For obvious reasons, a lancer will not attack a target directly in front of his horse, so the lance is aimed to one side of the horse's head, usually no more than 30° to either side of the direction of travel.

The horseman's lance first appeared in west and north Central Asia among the horse peoples of the Asian steppes. These horsemen have used the lance as their primary shock weapon almost since the domestication of the horse.[20] Both historical and experimental studies have shown that it is perfectly possible to successfully attack a solid target with a couched lance, bareback, let alone just without stirrups. As neither stirrups nor a saddle are essential for the effective use of the lance, the early riders of Central Asia adopted it very quickly.

Ayusi Dispersing Rebels with a Lance: Anyusi, a member of the Imperial Guard, won a great battle for the Qing army in 1755. Painting by Lang Shining (Chinese name of Giuseppe Castiglione, b. 1688). Collection of the National Palace Museum, Taiwan, Republic of China.

At first not more than 2 meters (6.5 ft) long, the lance increased gradually in length until the Sarmatian *kontus* or *contus sarmaticus* appears, which could be up to 4.5 meters (14.75 ft) long. These long shafts were provided with a leather loop or sling at the point of balance for carrying the weapon, and possibly as an aid when using it. The early spear heads used by these people had a long socket, fitting over the shaft almost to the point of the spear, forming a mid-rib with a blade on each side. As the lance shaft increased in length, the lance head did as well, and the socket no longer ran the full length of the blade.

This type of long lance continued in use by Parthian *cataphracti* or *clibanarii* at least into the 3rd century CE, and the Huns, Avars, and Mongols all used long lances in battle. The lance went through a number of changes in Europe during the Middle Ages, culminating in the heavy jousting lance. Lances used in warfare were lighter. For example, lances were the principal weapon of the Polish Husaria of the 16th and 17th century. Up to 5 meters (16.4 ft) long, these Husaria weapons were made of two pieces of wood, hollowed out for lightness. The shaft was round from the point back to a ball shaped hand guard, with a small octagonal section for a grip (Zygulski, 1975). The point was relatively small.

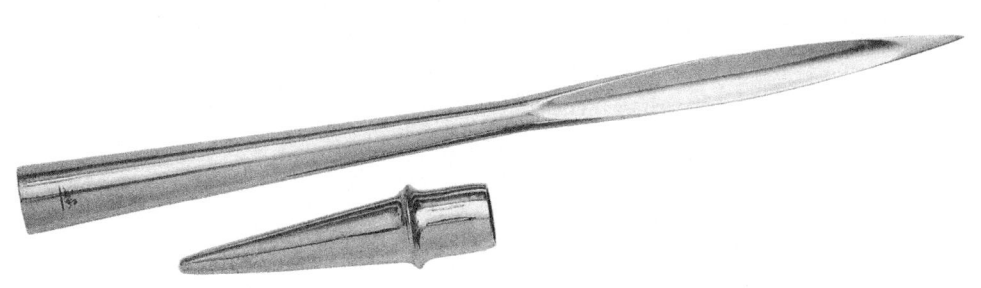

Lance head & butt: Replica of the British 1868 pattern, used with great effect by the cavalry untile the end of the century and still in ceremonial use today by the Canadian Mounted Police. Provided by CAS Iberia. www.casiberia.com Overall: 12.25" Blade: 5.75" Weight: 8.2oz

The lance suffered a brief eclipse in western warfare during the 17th and 18th centuries, but was reintroduced from Asia and remained in favor among European cavalry until the 20th century. British service lances of the 19th century had 2.75 meter (9 foot) shafts of either bamboo or ash, steel shoes and heads, and weighed from 1.9-2.3 Kg (4.25 to 5 pounds). The lance heads varied in length from 30 to 71 cm (12 to 28 inches), although in every case the sharp bladed portion probably did not exceed 18 cm (7 inches). These lances had a 33 cm (13 inch) sling bound onto the shaft for better retention in use and for carrying on parade.

The lance was the primary weapon of the *soldados cueros* on the Spanish Frontier in North America, and it was adopted by the Comanches, who made very effective use of it well into the 19th century. By the end of the 19th century, although it was quite obvious that cavalry no longer had any effective tactical role except as mounted infantry, conservative leadership everywhere tried to preserve the lance for the cavalry's most ineffective but glorious tactic, the mounted charge. Although it was much superior to the sword/saber as a primary cavalry weapon in a charge, reliance on any edged weapon was suicidal against an entrenched enemy armed with magazine rifles and machine guns.

Long infantry spears or pikes are highly specialized weapons, designed primarily to enable a tight infantry formation to hold off mounted shock troops, and they are a weapon of considerable antiquity. In the absence of effective firearms, they were the tactical solution to the problem of heavy cavalry armed with lances. The Minoans used extremely long pikes (Ferrill, 1985: 94). The Macedonian infantry *sarissa* was a two-handed pike some 4 meters (13 feet) long made of cornel wood (*Cornus spp.*) in two parts joined by a metal sleeve. It weighed about twelve pounds.

Tactically, fighting in very close order allowed pikemen to present a dense array of points toward any foe in an unbroken line, an effective barricade against cavalry, and extremely intimidating to other infantry. Nevertheless, dense pike formations have fatal disadvantages. They are unwieldy and easily by-passed, and are terribly vulnerable to missile weapons and flank attacks. Pike formations must be mixed with other weapons to survive. Alexander the Great understood this better than any other ancient general, and his pikemen were used as one component in combination with other weapons, but the traditional Greek phalanx suffered from these tactical problems, and the more flexible Roman formations destroyed them.

Pike formations came back into their own at the end of the Middle Ages, first used by the Swiss and then by the German *Landknechts*. The reintroduction of the pike by the Swiss came as a tactical surprise, and for a brief period pike formations dominated the unsophisticated battlefields of late medieval Europe. Swiss and *Landknecht* pike formations had a relatively short useful life. These Renaissance pike formations were vulnerable to disruption by archery, and then to Spanish tactics using sword and buckler to get past the points of the pikes. They offered fat, vulnerable targets to artillery and individual firearms when these weapons gradually became effective.

The tremendously long pike is heavy and unwieldy, burden enough without a shield, unnecessary in a dense pike formation and a hindrance to mobility. Nevertheless, spearmen or pikemen in ancient armies carried shields. Their presence in those formations is a small tactical puzzle. Really, when used in formation, the pike did away with the necessity for shields, and Swiss and *Landknecht* pikemen did not use shields. They were often mercenary units, and quick to avoid or discard anything useless. Their formations could be tighter without shields, increasing the density of points presented at an enemy.

The 17th century pike was very long, up to 6 meters (almost 20 feet) in length. The points were relatively small and not bladed although they often had extremely long languets. They normally possessed a spiked iron butt cap which helped to balance the unwieldy weapon, and allowed the butt to be held more firmly against the ground when repelling cavalry. There was usually a tassel or thong just above the place where the pike would rest upon the shoulder while marching. This was to allow rain water running down the pike to drain off to one side without soaking the pikeman.

The pike's only advantages were low cost and minimal training. The pike was a clumsy, inflexible weapon, limited technically for individual use and tactically for unit use. The pike is not designed for individual combat, as it may be easily grabbed or by-passed and at that point it is useless just long enough to be fatal to its owner. Each pikeman had to carry a sword or other sidearm for personal defense.

The final answer was to mix pikes with matchlock firearms, one protecting the other, and the pike survived in this role until the beginning of the 18th century, when it was finally replaced by the bayonet, a device to convert a muzzle-loading firearm into a clumsy thrusting spear to repel a cavalry charge. The modern bayonet has been retained largely for its "moral effect" and to intimidate civilians when military units are assigned to assist the civil authority for riot control. It is utterly useless in modern combat, something that has been known at least since the American Civil War (Jamieson, 1994: 11). It is the last and least effective of the military spears.

SPEARS AND THE ASIAN MARTIAL ARTS

Metals and Technology

However unlikely, it is possible that bronze metallurgy may have originated in China independently; as it may have done in the Americas about 900 years ago, long before the arrival of the Spanish. Nevertheless, we are compelled to conclude that the metal bladed thrusting spear and techniques for its use were introduced to the civilizations of the Far East through Central Asia from the Mediterranean, where bronze metallurgy and technology seems to have originated about 5000 years ago.

Bronze metallurgy did not appear in China for at least another 1500 years, and both Northeastern Iran and Central Asia lie between the eastern Mediterranean and China. This gives support to a supposition that the thrusting spear was introduced into the Far East from either Northeast Iran or Central Asia, perhaps through the region of the Altai Mountains or the Tarim Basin. Japan entered the bronze age fairly late, perhaps 1000 years after China, and we may tentatively suppose that both metallurgy and the bladed spear were introduced to Japan from China.

Later, iron working technology spread more rapidly than bronze technology, and it spread from a single source. Iron working was developed by the Hittites around 3500 YBP (years before the present) but was kept a closely guarded military secret. Iron technology eventually spread from Anatolia into eastern Europe, Central Asia, and the Middle East, but the spread was not even. The adoption of iron metallurgy by the Assyrians for the weapons carried by their armies 2700 to 2900 YBP may have been an important intermediary for the spread of iron weapons into Central Asia. The European Halstatt culture (ca. 2700 to 2900 YBP) is associated with the first European use of iron, and iron technology had reached Britain and Scandinavia by 2500 YBP. Iron technology reached China about the same time. It is possible, even probable, that iron metallurgy didn't reach some areas in Central Asia until 2200 YBP or later, although iron weapons undoubtedly did. We assume that the earlier bronze technology spread the same way, although more slowly.

China

The most important weapons in the Chinese military were the bow and arrow and the spear (*qiang*), and there were specialized bodies of soldiers trained to use each weapon. The spear remained a major military weapon up to the introduction of modern firearms in Chinese armies in the late 19th century. Chinese thrusting spears often have dense horse hair tuffs fastened to the shafts just below the blades. The idea is to keep blood from running down the shafts where it could interfere with the proper manipulation of the weapon.

At first glance, the spear in China appears to have achieved a complexity of form and technique unknown elsewhere. However, on closer inspection we find that many so-called spears are really different weapons. Halberds, glaives, long clubs, rakes, pitchforks, even shovels are often lumped into the spear category. It should be evident that this huge number of Chinese staff weapons, many of which are obviously *ad hoc* improvisations of agricultural implements for combat, are not all to be regarded as spears or as representative of true fighting arts. The unusual variety of such weapons reflects desperate measures for local defense during the prolonged periods of civil disorder so regrettably frequent in Chinese history. Analogous European weapons may be found associated with the various peasant uprisings between the French *Jacquerie* in 1358 and the German peasant revolt of 1525.

Even so, there were many different types of real spears used in China. During the Song Dynasty (960–1280), the Chinese tended to classify their spear types on the basis of appearance, not technique, although certain types were felt to be best for specific tactical situations. Although basically a simple weapon, the Chinese elaborated on the spear, adding various hooks and teeth to the blade. They developed complex techniques for the spear's use and various "schools" to teach the systems which "standardized" these techniques. During the Ming Dynasty (1368–1644), the pike made its appearance, as we have seen, a weapon very different from the ordinary spear, both in terms of its length and its small head.

The spear became a major civilian martial arts weapon, some instructors even regarding it as the fundamental weapon on which technique for all others was based. As we have seen, the immense antiquity of this weapon provides some justification for this attitude. *Xingyiquan*, the oldest of the internal Chinese martial arts was founded toward the end of the Ming Dynasty (1368–1644) by Ji Longfeng, a master of spear technique who based the principles of xingyiquan on his experience and knowledge of the spear (Kennedy & Guo, 2006). This is important verification of the central importance of the spear to the origin and development of all the fighting arts.

Illustrations found in the military arts manual by Chinese General Qi Jiguang (1507–1587) entitled the *Book of Effective Discipline*.

Illustrations on spear practice found in the military arts manual by Chinese General Qi Jiquang (1507–1587) entitled the *Book of Effective Discipline*.

From the Song (960–1280) through the Qing (1644–1911) there was a gradual reduction in both the length and weight of the long spear or pike. In the Qing, the barred spear became more common, although usually the bars were sharpened into side blades and during this period some spears were shortened to *assegai* length. As spears became shorter and lighter, they became easier to manipulate and possibilities for the elaboration of technique increased. This was reflected in the increase in the number of different "schools" of spear fighting, also indicative of fierce competition for students and adherents during this period.

The Chinese have developed a number of fascinating spear drills and exercises in their efforts to wring all the possibilities out of this versatile weapon. Much of what was taught during the Qing may be seen as unnecessarily complicated and recherché. However, these complexities are indicative of a really thorough exploration of the spear's technical possibilities for an individual in both offense and defense.

The tantalizing samples of spear forms in Asmolov (1993)[21] indicate that traditional Chinese techniques were practical and effective, but they differ markedly from those practiced in modern wushu spear exercises. Sadly, the modern practice no longer reflects a real understanding of the weapon's practical utility. The modern Chinese wushu spear is long, light weight, and flexible, and it differs so greatly from other spears as almost to require treatment as a separate weapon.

Modern wushu techniques are gymnastic exercises (Qiu, 1999: 2) which require marvelous dexterity and physical skill. The practitioner may spin in position, jump into the air, and may even throw his spear above his head, catching it in a favorable position for executing his next technique. A characteristic feature of wushu spear technique is the rapid rotation of the spear point, impossible without a very flexible shaft. Other techniques require a very low density shaft material, especially the one-handed thrust holding the shaft at its very end with the arm fully extended. These visually impressive techniques are splendidly demonstrated by Master Hung Tingseng in his performance of the Mi Zu Men Six Harmony Spear form.

The wushu spear shaft appears to be of "white wax wood," which is flexible, tough, low density, and has a natural taper. Along with a small spear head, these properties allow the modern wushu practitioner to perform demanding and intricate techniques impossible with a heavier weapon. The tassel fixed to the shaft just below the head is no longer useful as a device to keep blood from running down the shaft and making it hard to grip. It does make it easier to keep track of the pointed end during the rapid manipulations of the weapon and enhances the visual effect of the performance.

Bajiquan's Big Spear Techniques

- shaking   dou   抖
- collapsing   beng   崩
- stabbing   ci   刺
- spiralling, entangling   chan   纏
- turning & pressing   ya   呀
- poking   tong   桶

Big spear training exercises performed by Tony Yang. Selected photographs taken from a previously published article: Figler, R., and Yang, T. (2000). Bajiquan & Piguazhang, part II: Foundational training methods. *Journal of Asian Martial Arts*, 9(1): 16–33. Photographs courtesy of T. Yang.

"White wax wood" is often wrongly identified as coming from *Ligustrum lucidum* (Chinese privet) in the Oleaceae family. Samples sent to the USDA Forest Service Forest Products Laboratory in Madison, WI were identified as coming from *Fraxinus floribunda*, Wallich, an ash. The genus *Fraxinus* is also in the Oleaceae family, but growth characteristics and mechanical properties make ash a much more suitable spear shaft wood than privet. In fact ash is highly regarded as a material for staves, impact tool and weapon handles, and spear shafts everywhere it is found.

Japan

Japanese spears and techniques for their use, *sojutsu*, would appear to be a development of early Chinese weapons and technique with subsequent Chinese influence at different periods. Almost all techniques are performed with two hands, using the underhand thrust as the basic position. Shields were normally not used.

The bronze *dohoko*, a spear with a socketed blade about a foot long, is the oldest bladed weapon of Japan. The blade retained its characteristic shape as the *hoko* after it was made of iron, and sometimes possessed a hook on one side which may turn up or down. It remained the standard spear until the late Heian (794–1185 CE) or early Kamakura (1185–1333 CE) periods. Shortly after the battle of Kurikara in 1183, the *hoko* seems to have been eclipsed as a weapon by the *naginata*, a type of glaive, a very different pole arm, not a spear. The disappearance of this useful and inexpensive weapon and its development into the *yari* require explanation.

Yari and end cap. Design based on original dating to feudal Japan.
Overall: 79" Blade: 16.75" Wt: 3lbs 11oz
Provided by CAS Iberia. www.casiberia.com

The spear reappeared as a combat arm about 150 years later, possibly at the battle of Kamakura in 1333. It had changed in the interim to become the tanged *yari* or *su-yari* (a spear with a tanged head). This spear was the least expensive edged weapon to make and one of the most effective on any battlefield. After 1333, it was most commonly carried by the non-samurai, lower class soldiers, the *ashigaru*.

By that period, the Japanese samurai had already adopted the superb swords which were to be their basic weapon—the hallmark and symbol of their warrior status. The *yari* was adopted by the monks of the Buddhist militant orders (the *sohei*), as their principal weapon, and they developed superior techniques for its use. By the Muromachi period (1392–1573), the samurai had again adopted the spear as a major weapon and *sojutsu* appeared.[22] The monks no longer dominated spear technique. Then in 1571, Nobunaga Oda smashed the *sohei* monks and destroyed their monasteries.

The matchlock musket was introduced into Japan around the middle of the 16th century, and it was quickly and widely adopted. The remarkable trio of Nobunaga Oda, Hideyoshi Toyotomi, and Tokugawa Ieyasu, who unified Japan, experimented with pike and shot mixtures similar to those used in Europe. The surviving examples of spears with very long shafts from 4.5 to 5.5 meters (14-3/4 to 18 feet) long probably date from this period. The successful tactics used by Nobunaga at the battle of Nagashino in 1575 could easily have resulted from experiments with such a mix of weapons.

The *yari* is the classical spear of Japan, and so deserves a description in some detail. However, there was a great deal of variation in design, so we can only describe its average characteristics. The *su-yari* has a pointed double-edged blade with a pronounced spine on one or, more usually, both sides. The point section is usually short, and the edges are straight and parallel for most of their length. The edges end in a constriction which forms a round or polygonal neck. The base of this neck rests against the top of the wooden shaft and serves to spread the force of impact across the entire cross-section of the shaft. There is a long integral tang below the base which is held in the shaft by as many as four pegs. The shaft is reinforced to prevent splitting. Crossbars, when present, may be separate or integral to the lower blade or neck, and may be sharpened to form edged hooks. Once again, there is enormous variation in design. The shaft of *shira kashi*, or Japanese white oak[23] (*Quercus myrsinifolia*, Blume) averages about 2.5 to 3 meters (8.25 to 9.75 feet) in length and generally possesses a metal butt cap on the distal end.

Illustration from *Tales of the Hermit, Vol. II*, by Oscar Ratti and Adele Westbrook. © 2002 Futuro Designs & Publications

After the battle of Sekigahara (15 September 1600), the spear faded in importance as Japan entered the long Tokugawa period of relative peace. Although there are at least six schools (*ryuha*) teaching *sojutsu* in Japan today, there are only about 1000 practitioners. The oldest extant Japanese martial tradition is the Tenshin Shoden Katori Shinto-Ryu and it teaches *sojutsu* only as advanced technique. *Sojutsu* never developed into a modern budo form.

Concluding Remarks

The spear is very old, possibly the oldest and therefore the most basic of all human weapons. A very early tool for gathering food, then perhaps a crude hunting weapon, it was eclipsed by the javelin, only to reappear when lithic and then bronze technology made useful bladed spearheads possible. Basic thrusting spear technique was developed for use against dangerous large game and predators. The bladed thrusting spear was man's first tool designed to put protective distance between the individual and a dangerous antagonist, whether animal or human. Nevertheless, until the development of metallurgy, the spear was still a weapon of desperation when used in self-defense.

Both the spear and the techniques for its use were first developed by hunters and later adapted for human combat and warfare. There was a close relationship between hunting and warfare which lasted into the 20th century. When the spear was adapted for personal combat, tactical considerations led to increasing sophistication of technique, which reached its highest development in East Asia. The spear has two ends, and it may be used with staff techniques as well as for slashing and thrusting.

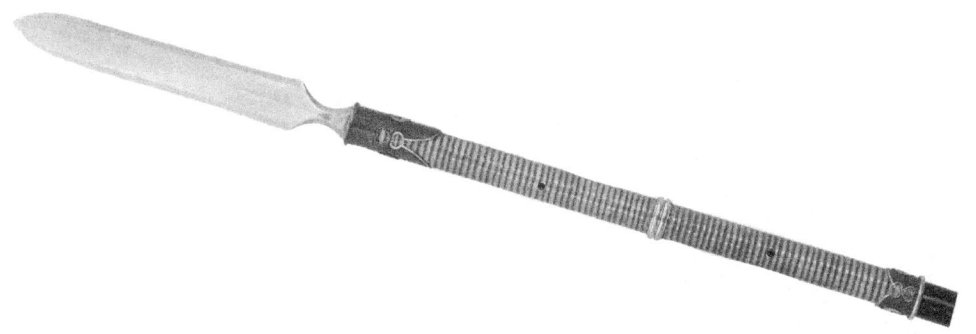

Yari.
Design based on original dating to feudal Japan.
Overall: 73.25" Blade: 11" Wt: 3lbs 1oz
Provided by CAS Iberia. www.casiberia.com

Although the shield might have been developed for additional protection against dangerous animals, it very likely appeared after the spear became a weapon for personal combat. In any event, the thrusting spear was then used in combination with the shield, and the presence of a shield on one arm inhibited the development of fighting technique with the spear in Europe. The development of spear technique there was also retarded by its adoption for use in unison by large numbers of warriors in close formation. The spear's use as a unit weapon rather than an individual one further reduced the possible variety of individual technique, led to longer and longer spear shafts, to the increased importance of shields, and eventually to the relatively static pike.

As projectile weapons appeared and became more and more effective, they further widened the protective distance between an individual and a hostile target and became preferred over the spear. However, it was not until the heavy caliber personal firearm became truly dependable that the spear finally lost its preeminence as a protective weapon.

Notes

1. Note here that no radiometric dating techniques were used. The dating must be considered as an estimate only. Getting comprehensive information on the local stratigraphy of the area; who did the work and when, etc. etc. etc. might be difficult. (Meaningful radiometric dating of buried material in the 300K to 500K year range requires the serendipitous occurrence of exactly the right natural material–seldom happens! [personal communication, John C. Dohrenwend, Ph.D.])
2. Recent discoveries indicate that both *H. neanderthalensis* (back to as far as 250–350 thousand years ago) and *H. heidelbergensis* (back to as far as 600 thousand years ago) had the capacity for complex, organized speech.
3. Even well studied areas are sometimes a source of new data requiring that we rethink our ideas of early man and his distribution and evolution. See: S.A. Parfitt et al. (1997), and R. Dennell and W. Roebroeks (2005).
4. Site factors related to the preservation and stratigraphy of the samples to be found there.
5. The spectral response of the human eye strongly suggests a long period of adaptation in heavy closed canopy vegetation, perhaps gallery forests along rivers cutting through prairie or savannah?

6. The best popular exposition of the evidence supporting this controversial hypothesis was that written by Elaine Morgan in 1990. Since that book was written, new evidence has been discovered which supports that hypothesis (see: Macaulay, et al, 2005). It certainly offers the best description today of man's spread into the western hemisphere (Dixon, 1999).
7. The extrapolation of this observed modern hunting technique to the deep past is a plausible and attractive hypothesis, but it is still no more than that.
8. Although modern man has few anatomical or physiological adaptations which would fit him for existence in a grasslands biome, those few are very interesting. Modern man has musculature adapted to permit him to run for long distances at paces of 15 to 10 minutes per mile, 1.8 to 2.7 msec-1 (4 to 6 mph). Furless modern man can dump heat very effectively by sweating. To do so, he needs water, a lot of water. Once more, proximity to water seems to be critical to human evolution.
9. The geological Quaternary period (1.65 million years ago to the present) roughly corresponds to the paleontologist's Pleistocene epoch, defined as ending about 10,000 years ago.
10. Properly mounted to expose only their sharp edges.
11. European Middle Ages date from the fall of the western Roman Empire in 476 to ca. 1400 CE.
12. Up to $1,700.00 USD or 1300 Euros.
13. Estimates vary.
14. Neanderthal men are present in the archeological record from roughly 500 thousand to about 24–26 thousand years ago. Most recent dates from Findlayson et al. 2006.
15. Dating is very rough for the somewhat enigmatic Heidelberg man, roughly 800– 600 to 100 thousand years ago, or even perhaps present more recently.
16. This is no longer an Olympic requirement.
17. However, recent studies indicate that bronze armor wasn't that good, and leather armor was both less expensive, more effective, and much more common.
18. Tougher than the original stuff, I might add.
19. Pottery decorations often show Greeks shown using spears in obvious overhand motion. Thrust or throw? Artistic conventions are not clear.
20. The lance is a much more effective weapon for mounted warriors than any sword, and for most of the history of horse soldiers, the sword/saber was a secondary weapon.
21. Regrettably, the text is in Russian, a language still opaque to me.
22. The Chinese character for "yari" may also be read as "so", therefore the art of

the spear is known as "sojutsu."

[23] Actually, this species is not a "white oak' but an evergreen oak with remarkably tough wood, prized by musicians for drum sticks.

Bibliography

Akeley, C. (1923). *In brightest Africa*. Garden City. NY: Doubleday.

Anderson, J. (1985). *Hunting in the ancient world*. Berkeley, CA: University of California Press.

Asmolov, K. (1993). *Istoria kholodnogo oruzhiye (History of cold steel): The East and the Occident: Part I*. Book 5 in the series: *Taŭnia voinskikh iskusstv (Secret fighting arts)*. Moscow. Published by the Medical and Scientific Information Center "National Health" and the "Choy Dao" International Association of Fighting Arts. Section: "Vlastelin vsego oruzhiye" (Master of all weapons): 110–137.

Bise, G. (1984). *The hunting book*, by Gaston Phoebus. (J. Peter Tallon, Trans.). London: Regent Books/Hightext.

Bickerstaff, I. (1999). *The heritage of the longbow*. Privately published in Great Britain.

Blackmore, H. (1971). *Hunting weapons*. New York: Walker & Company.

Boddington, C. (2002). *The perfect shot, North America: Shot placement for North American big game*. Long Beach, CA: Safari Press.

Bramble, D., & Lieberman, D. (18 November 2004). Endurance running and the evolution of homo. *Nature, 432*(7015), 345.

Brentjes, B. (1996). *Arms of the sakas*. Varanasi, India: Rishi Publications.

Bruhn de Hoffmeyer, A. (1972). *Arms & armour in Spain, A short survey. The bronze age to the end of the high middle ages, Vol I*. Instituto de Estudios Sobre Armas Antiguas. Madrid.

Bruhn de Hoffmeyer, A. (1982). *Arms & armour in Spain, A short survey. Vol II. From the end of the 12th century to the beginning of the 15th century*. Instituto de Estudios Sobre Armas Antiguas. Madrid.

Caras, R. (1964). *Dangerous to man*. New York: Chilton.

Carrier, D. (1984). The energetic paradox of human running and hominid evolution. *Current Anthropology, 25*(4), 483–495.

Coles, J. (1973). *Archeology by experiment*. New York: Scribners.

Coon, C. (1971). *The hunting peoples*. Boston: Atlantic-Little-Brown.

Cummins, J. (1988). *The hound and the hawk: The art of medieval hunting*. New York: St. Martins.

Dennell, R. (27 Feb. 1997). The world's oldest spears. *Nature, 385*(6619), 767–768.

Dennell, R., & Roebroeks, W. (29 December 2005). An Asian perspective on early human dispersal from Africa. *Nature, 438*(7070), 1099–1104.

Dixon, E. (1999). *Bones, boats, & bison*. Albuquerque, NM: University of New Mexico Press.

Draeger, D., & Smith, R. (1980). *Comprehensive Asian fighting arts*. Tokyo: Kodansha. Pages 109–113 Japan; 151–152 India; 174–175 Malaya; 185–186 Philippines.

Elgood, R. (1994). *The arms and armour of Arabia*. Aldershot: Scholar Press.

Ellehauge, M. (1948). *The spear: Traced through its post-Roman development*. Copenhagen: Tøjhusmuseets Skrifter 5. N. Olaf Møller.

Ferrill, A. (1985). *The origins of war: From the stone age to Alexander the Great*. New York: Thames and Hudson.

Filipiak, K. (2001). *Die Chinesische kampfkunst*. Leipzig: Leipziger Universitatsverlag.

Findlayson, et al. (19 October 2006). Late survival of the Neanderthals at the southernmost extreme of Europe. *Nature, 443*(7113), 850–853.

Frison, G. (2004). *Survival by hunting*. Berkeley, CA: University of California Press.

Froissart. J. (1901). *Chronicles*. (T. Johnes, Trans.). London: Colonial Press.

Gabriel, R., & Metz, K. (1991). *From Sumer to Rome: The Military capabilities of ancient armies*. New York: Greenwood Press.

Griffith, P. (1995). *The Viking art of war*. London: Greenhill.

Hanson, V. (1989). *The Western way of war*. Berkeley, CA: California University Press.

Hung, Tingseng (2004). *Mi zu men six harmony spear*. DVD. Made in China, released through Tsunami Productions.

Hunter, J. (1952). *Hunter*. New York: Harper & Brothers.

Jameison, P. (1994). *Crossing the deadly ground*. Tuscaloosa, AL: University of Alabama Press.

Kauffman, S. (November 2006). The evolution of future wealth. *Scientific American, 295*(5), 44.

Kennedy, B., & Guo, E. (2006). Jack Dempsey: Master of xingyiquan. *Classical Fighting Arts, 10*, 31–36

Kizu, Yasu (1990). *Japanese spears*. Hollywood, CA: Hawley Publications.

Knecht, H. (1997). *Projectile technology*. (Interdisciplinary Contributions to Archeology). New York: Plenum Publishing.

Knutsen, R., & Knutsen, P. (2004). *Japanese spears*. Honolulu, HI: University of Hawai'i Press.

Kurten, B., & Anderson, E. (1987). *Pleistocene mammals of North America*. New

York: Columbia University Press.

Lebedynsky, I. (1990). *Les armes cosaques et caucasiens*. La Tour Du Pin, France: Editions du Portail.

Lebedynsky, I. (1992). *Les armes orientales*. La Tour Du Pin, France: Editions du Portail.

Macaulay, V., et. al. (13 May 2005). Single, rapid coastal settlement of Asia revealed by analysis of complete mitochondrial genomes. *Science*, 30(5724): 1034–1036.

Mails, T. (1972). *Mystic warriors of the great plains*. Garden City, NY: Doubleday.

Manfred, F. (1954). *Lord grizzly*. New York: McGraw-Hill.

Mannix, D. (1978). *The wolves of Paris*. New York: Dutton. (Avon edition, 1979)

Marshall, E. (1957). *Shikar and safari: Jungle hunting thrills*. New York: Dell.

Mason, O. (2002). *Aboriginal American harpoons: A study in ethnic distribution and invention*. (Reproduction of Smithsonian Edition, 1900). Honolulu, HI: University Press of the Pacific.

McGhee, R. (1996). *Ancient people of the arctic*. Vancouver, BC: University of British Columbia Press.

Morgan, E. (1990). *The scars of evolution*. Oxford: Oxford University Press.

Morris, D. (1965). *The washing of the spears*. New York: Simon and Schuster.

Morris, E. (2003). *Hunting with spears*. St. Cloud, MN: MK Publishing.

Poortvleit, R. (1994). *Journey to the ice age*. New York: Harry N. Abrams.

Pope, S. (1926). *The adventurous bowmen*. New York: G.P. Putnam's Sons.

Qiu, Pixiang (1999). *Basic spear play* (Chinese Wushu Series). Beijing: Foreign Language Press.

Siemel, S. (1953). *Tigrero!* New York: Prentice Hall.

Skennerton, I. (1994). *British service sword and lance patterns*. Privately published in Australia.

Stone, G. (1934). A glossary of the construction, decoration and use of arms and armor. New York: Jack Brussel. Reprint 1961.

Thieme, H. (27 February 1997). Lower paleolithic hunting spears from Germany. *Nature*, 385(6619), 807–810.

Underwood, R. (1999). *Anglo-Saxon weapons and warfare*. Stroud UK: Tempus.

Wagner, E. (1979). *European weapons and warfare*. London: Octopus/Mayflower.

White, S. (1979). *Lions in the path*. Prescott, AZ: Wolfe Publishing. 1987 (1926).

Yang, J. (1999). *Ancient Chinese weapons*. Boston: YMAA.

Zygulski, Jr., Zdzislaw (1975). *Bron w dawnej Polski*. Warsaw, Poland: Panstwowe Wydawnictwo Naukowe.

index

Africa, 3, 15, 90
Akamine, Eiiryo, 32
Alcázar, Siege of, 3
Aljubarrota, Battle of, 3
antler, 87, 95
archery, 1, 4, 18, 110
arnis, 42, 58
Assyria, 2, 111
atlatl, 100–101
Aztecs, 3, 100
bajiquan, 116
Balearic, 3, 7, 13, 18–19
Bartitsu, 56–57
Barton-Wright, E.W., 56–57
bone, 77, 87
bow, 1–3, 17, 26, 98, 100–101, 112
Britain, 55, 82 note 1, 112
bronze, 13, 87–88, 92, 101–103, 111–112, 117, 119, 121 note 17
Canary Islands, 3
Castilians, 3
Central Asia, 3–4, 99, 108, 111–112
chikusaji, 30, 49 note 2
China, 3, 24–25, 36–37, 39–41, 43–44, 46–47, 49 note 11, 111–112
Chinen, Masami, 31
Chinen, Pechin, 31
Chinen, Sanda, 31–32
Chodo, Oshiro, 31
crossbar, 87–88, 92, 95, 97, 118
Demura, Fumio, 32
dogs, 52, 54, 69–70, 74–75, 80–81, 91, 96–98
Egypt, 2, 18, 101
England, 3, 89
eskrima/esgrima, 42, 58
espada y daga, 42
Gilman, Michael, 61–63
Greek, 2, 7, 92, 98, 102–105, 110, 121 note 19
guai gun, 59
Gushikawa, Tiragwa, 31
Hamahiga Peichin, 30, 33, 48
hapkido, 58–59

Hasekura, Tsunenaga, 42
Heinrich VII, 3
Hejaz, 3
Henry VIII, 100
Hideyoshi, Toyotomi, 118
Higa, Matsu (Royal Bodyguard), 32, 35
Higa, Seitoku, 31
Huguenots, 3
Huang Tingseng, 115
Husaria, 108
Incas, 3
Index of Relative Theoretical Lethality (IRTL), 16
India, 3, 24, 36–37, 40, 46, 58, 104
Indonesia, 3, 24, 36–40, 41, 46, 65
Inoue, Motokatsu, 32
iron/steel, 26, 43–45, 47, 67, 94, 99, 102, 110–112, 117
Isa, Kaishu (aka, Isa Shinyu), 32
Italy, 3, 7, 55
Ji, Longfeng, 113
Jordan, 3
jutte/jitte, 30, 36–37
Kankushiku, Sanda (a.k.a., Kangusuku Ufuchiku), 32–33
Kenshinjan Shorin-Ryu, 32, 35
Kina, Shosei, 32–33
kobudo, 30, 33, 34, 36, 46–47, 49 note 5, 75
Korea, 3, 36–37, 39, 43, 58
Kukishin-Ryu, 58
la canne, 57, 68
Louis XIV, 3
Mabuni, Kenwa, 32
Macao, 41
Malaysia, 3, 36–37
manji-sai, 28, 36, 40
Matayoshi, Shinko, 31
Matayoshi, Shinpo, 31, 39
Maximilian I, 100
Meiji Restoration, 25, 47
Mexico, 3, 90, 100
Mi Zu Men Six Harmony Spear, 115
Mongols, 3, 108

Murakami, Katsumi, 32
Nobunaga, Oda, 118
naginata, 117
Nago Chogen, Prince, 30
Nájera, 3
Nakazato, Shugoro, 31
nunchaku, 75
nunte, 28, 36, 48
Okinawa, 24–25, 29–48, 75
Palestine, 3
pentjak-silat, 38
Persia, 2, 7, 15, 100
Peru, 3
Philippines, 3, 36, 42, 46, 58
pilum, 99
Poland, 15
Portuguese, 40–41
projectiles, 1, 5–21, 87, 99, 120
Qi Jiguang, 113–114
rate of fire, 15–16
Roman, 3, 5, 7, 14, 18, 19, 54, 93, 97–99, 105, 111, 121 note 11
saijutsu, 30, 34–35, 43–44
Sakagami, Ryusho, 32, 37, 39–40, 43
Sakugawa, Kanga "Tode", 31–33
Sancerre, siege of, 3
Satsuma, 25, 30, 36, 44, 45, 47
Satsuma weapons ban, 47
savate, 57
Sekigahara, battle of, 119
shield, 17, 94, 98–99, 101–105, 107, 110, 117, 120
Shindo Muso-Ryu, 59
Shitahaku, Oyakata, 31, 33, 48, 49 note 12
Sho Shin, King, 30
Sho Tei, King, 31

Siemel, Alexander Sasha, 96–97
sling throwing techniques, 5–7
sling slope effect, 10
sohei, 117–118
sojutsu, 117–119, 121 note 22
Spanish, 3, 36, 40, 42, 100, 109–111
staff (bo), 30, 35, 36, 38, 45, 54, 58, 95, 101, 105, 112, 119
Sumerians, 101
sword cane, 79–80
Syria, 3
taijiquan, 59, 61–63
Taira, Shinken, 28, 33, 49 note 12
Tawada, Shimbuku, 31
Tedeschi, Marc, 59–61, 68
Tenshin Shoden Katori Shinto-Ryu, 119
tepki, 36
Tibet, 3, 14
tjabang (or cabang), 36–38
Tokugawa, Ieyasu, 118
tonfa, 45
trisula, 36–37
Tsaidam Basin, 3
Uchida-Ryu, 59
Uchida, Ryugoro, 59
Uechi, Kanei, 32
Uechi-Ryu, 32
ufuchiku, 30, 33, 49 note 2
umbrella, 80
Vigny, Pierre, 57–58
Viking, 94, 106
Visigoths, 3, 100
xingyiquan, 113
Yabiku, Moden, 32–33
Yara, Chatan, 31, 33, 49 note 5
yari, 117–119, 121 note 22
yawara, 69, 83 note 7

Printed in Great Britain
by Amazon